Cooking Wild

by Mark Roberts

Cooking Wild

Mark Roberts

Cooking Wild

First published in Great Britain in 2023 by
Bannister Publications Ltd.
118 Saltergate, Chesterfield, Derbyshire S40 1NG

Copyright © Mark Roberts
Illustrations by Becky Hague ©
ISBN: 978-1-909813-81-6

The moral rights of the author have been asserted.
All rights reserved.

A catalogue record for this book is available from the British Library
No part of this book may be reproduced in any form or by any
electronic or mechanical means, including information storage
and retrieval systems, without written permission from the author.

Printed and bound in Great Britain.

This book was self-published by Bannister Publications.
For more information on self-publishing visit:

www.bannisterpublications.com

Foreword

Writing a book about any subject is a brave thing to do. It is a lot of work and you can't help thinking it'll never be good enough; Mark has taken the bull by the horns here and written something very interesting. In part, this is a lovely little book designed to help you get creative and enjoy the outdoors, and in another, it is an encouragement to get involved with a wild larder. It also pays as a tribute to his father, whose passion for cooking has obviously been such an influence on Mark's food experience.

To write such a personal book and fill it with such obvious devotion is a grand achievement. Some fun recipes and some really beautiful drawings lend an air of timelessness to this little collection.

Enjoy it for what it is; I certainly did.

Tim Maddams
Private Chef, Writer, Cookery Teacher and Presenter.

"Marks journey to push the boundaries by combining his love of cooking and adventure to help others produce fantastic food, makes us very proud to be part of this project."

Ed
Chefslocker.

Foreword

An awesome book to accompany any adventure!

It's extremely refreshing to see that food can be created in any wild environment, without the need to stay at home and be in the kitchen!

Mark has most definitely broadened my horizons with his unique ideas on what can be done in the outdoors with very little fuss needed.

When undertaking a remote trek, it can often be easy to let a healthy diet slip. But this book has certainly given me a taste of what can be done to change that.

Make sure to add 'Cooking Wild' to your outdoor kit list!

Chaz Powell
Explorer of the Year 2021 – Expedition Leader – Ranger – Survivalist – FRGS.

Who's this for

This book is for everyone who loves food, has a sense of adventure and always watched those big budget cooking programs wishing they could create the perfect dish top chefs present to them under the glitz, glamour and lights of TV.

I wanted to create a book of recipe's, ideas and techniques that you can use no matter what your budget, size of cooking space or multiple ovens, hobs, microwaves and grills.

I have aimed to use as little utensils, pots, pans and cooking appliances as possible but not only that all my dishes will be prepped, cooked, plated and most importantly eaten outdoors, hopefully showing that if I can produce great tasting and great looking food in the wild you can produce it easily in the comfort of your own kitchen.

You will find no exact science, no exact measurements and no exact weights in this book. Each recipe is only a guide you can hopefully get ideas and inspiration from, and you can put your own stamp on creating your own wild dishes.

I have used as many natural ingredient's as possible, using sustainable food sources and as fresh as possible with guides and pointers where and when and how you can find your ingredient's if you want to avoid the big supermarkets.

To prove my point about being able to produce these dishes without unlimited resources and budgets I have cooked every one of these recipes in a different "wild" location.

So, whether it's perched on a rocky coastal shoreline, a nature filled woodland, the summit of a Scottish mountain, a white sandy beach, the baron moorlands of a National Park right through to the bottom of my humble garden we can all eat visually appealing, delicious, and nutritious food no matter how wild the location! Each recipe will be accompanied by information on the location filmed and illustrations.

You can find lots of these recipe's cooked on location in the wild with all the problems I faced free on my YouTube channel Wildernessrobbo.

About the author

My name is Mark Roberts, I'm a dad to my 2 sons Samuel and Samson, stepdad to Sydney, husband to my wife and best friend Becky, brother to Steve, Uncle to Amelia and son to my parents John and Maggie or as I like to call them Mum and Dad. I am a landscape gardener and Fire Fighter with a huge passion for the great outdoors and everything that goes with it. There are many inspirational quotes out there, some more famous than others and some will have more meaning than others. I have a few in throughout this book that I personally find meaning and inspiration from, the first one id like to share is by Mark Twain

"Twenty years from now you will be more disappointed by the things that you didn't do than by the ones you did do, so throw off the bowlines, sail away from the safe harbour, catch the trade winds in your sails. Explore, Dream, Discover."

- Mark Twain

I've spent almost all of my life in Chesterfield, Derbyshire. The Peak District and surrounding towns and villages are a fantastic place to grow up and live. It has an abundance of history, countryside, stately homes, attractions and small businesses. The Peak District is an upland area in England at the southern end of the Pennines. Mostly in Derbyshire, it includes parts of Cheshire, Greater Manchester, Staffordshire, West Yorkshire and South Yorkshire. It includes the Dark Peak, where most moorland is found and the geology gritstone, and the White Peak, a limestone area of valleys and gorges cutting the limestone plateau. The Dark Peak forms an arc on the north, east and west sides; the White Peak covers the central and southern tracks. It is home to an amazing amount of British wildlife with some great opportunities to see wild deer and owls. There are many popular walks including Curbar edge and the bleak but atmospheric plateau of Kinder Scout. As a child my parents would often take us for a walk on a Sunday afternoon through the stunning grounds of Chatsworth, along the river at Bakewell filled with hungry trout and circular walks around Ladybower and Linacre reservoir. These walks would often start out as an hours stroll but end up being a few hours hike due to my dad's famous 'detours'.

Growing up I've always loved the outdoors, wildlife, camping and adventures but like most young people, I never really appreciated food properly straight away, all I wanted was to eat well and then carry on with whatever it was I wanted to do next. Mealtimes at home, although important to my parents and we always sat at the family table, were for me merely a set time in the day, usually 6pm where we all sat down for tea before carrying on with our own jobs, hobbies, tasks, or leisure activities. As a family we used to holiday every summer in France on large campsites, fully set up family tents with whistling kettles a basic gas cooking hob and a set of plastic table and chairs outside. It was my brother and I's job each morning to walk to the camp shop and buy the fresh baguette and croissants for breakfast that we would often nibble the end off whilst walking back to the tent. Another holiday favourite was to walk along the French pine wood that led to the beach collecting pinecones as we walked. We would pick a spot either in the woods or on the sand dunes and tuck into a hot "poulet et pommes frites" or chicken and chips as we would say.

The earliest interest in food other than just eating it was with my dad, who has worked in hospitality and catering since the age of 14, he was working at a local catering college at the time. I had accompanied him to work one day avoiding school for a reason I can't remember, however during the day my dad took me down to the college's kitchen where I was faced with a piece of machinery I'd never seen before, a potato rumbler! All you did was throw a potato in what looked like a silver cement mixer, turn it on, a rumbling noise happened and then out popped a perfectly peeled potato! I thought it was great and must have peeled a whole sack full before I had to stop.

This was the start of my interest in food and many years down the line learning skills both at home and in a professional kitchen I now combine the love of the outdoors and the love of cooking and try to produce as many tasty meals outside as possible as I'm a firm believer in that not only cooking but eating outside taste better!

Dedication

At this point I would like to acknowledge and dedicate this book to the person who has taught me so much in this field, most of the time without realising due to the fact I'm not very good at following instructions so I'd watch, spy and learn from a distance while he cooked elaborate, posh, tasty, beautiful food for guests and family. I eventually went onto work alongside him in a successful London chef school. When I say worked alongside, I mean he ran the whole place, and I was the kitchens pot wash and dog's body. However, my time to work alongside him did eventually come when he owned his own hotel restaurant where he was Head Chef with myself as Sous-Chef. We covered breakfast, lunch and dinner service together as a duo producing good quality and well-presented food. Our crowning moment was serving two full restaurant sittings for the Christmas menu meal with obviously help from the front of house staff including my mum and brother. He has achieved many accolades and successes during his long and varied catering, hospitality and marketing career and continues to inspire and help the industry to date. He has worked both here in the UK for charities and overseas projects in such places as Sri Lanka and Bangladesh. He is extremely well thought of and respected throughout the industry working and liaising with many world-famous chefs and industry leaders. This however has not stopped him taking part and helping out with catering whenever possible at friends and family celebrations, local school events running a pancake stand, church gatherings, helping out on burger vans when events have been short staffed and getting involved with the camp food at youth organisations. This person is of course John Roberts, but to me, he's my dad.

"Thanks for everything Dad"

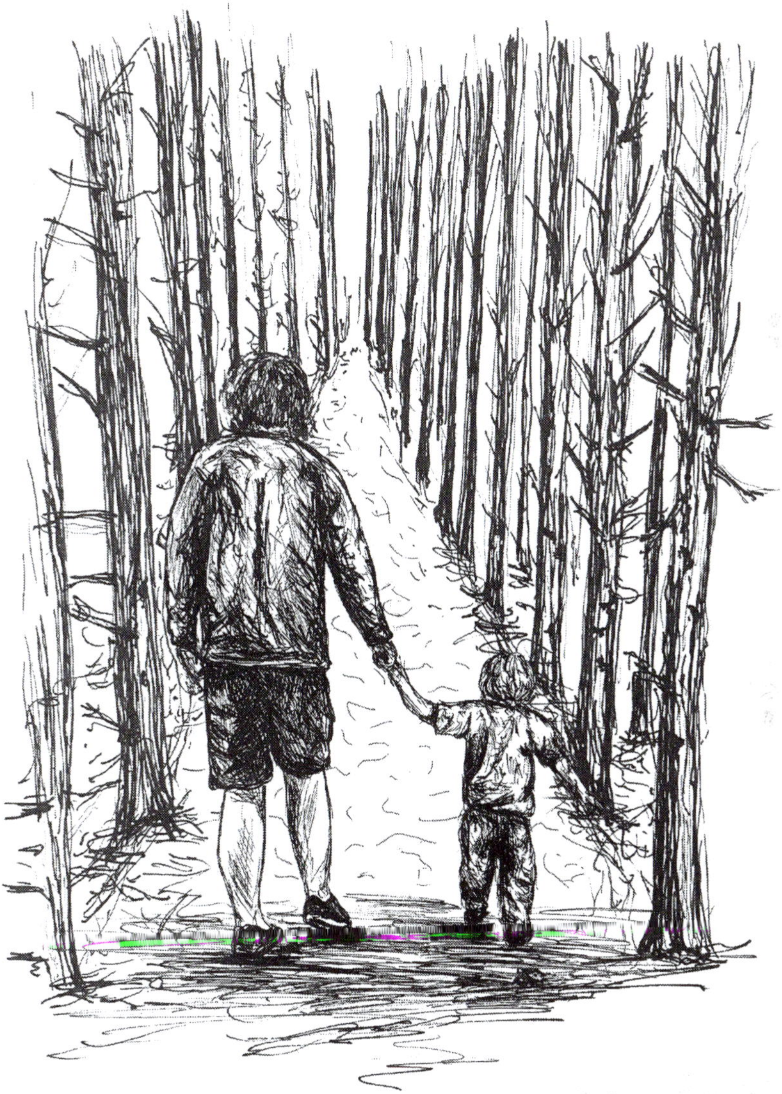

Words of wisdom

Wherever possible I always like to, and I encourage you to use food and produce that is as fresh, sustainable, and as ethical as possible. If that means a single line caught trout, rough shot game, free range poultry, home grown fruit and vegetables, foraged mushrooms and wild garlic or even finding a really good local farm shop that sells its own produce. I promise that not only the taste will be massively superior to any mass produced, chemically enhanced vegetables, or overcrowded, cramped animal sheds with no room to exercise, but you will be supporting the local farmers and encouraging better animal welfare.

Despite thoroughly enjoying my fruit and veg, I don't claim to be a vegan or vegetarian, however that does not mean I support the unnecessary cruelty and abuse some of the world's farmed animals are subject to. There is simply no need!

I hope this book encourages you to source great ingredients that have been produced ethically and sustainably after all your eating it so it's only right to want to know that your cauliflower hasn't been continually sprayed with chemicals or that your chicken hasn't been stuck in a crowded barn walking and sitting in not only its own faeces but a further 15000 chicken's faeces. An important lesson I have always taught my children is understanding where their food comes from. The saying "field to fork" and "kill it, cook it, eat it" are used regularly in our house. You'll be surprised how many young people of today couldn't even tell you what animal their beef burger came from or where the main ingredient from shepherd's pie comes from. We don't need the pallet of a Michelin starred chef but to understand and respect where the food we are eating is from a little more I feel would go along way in us eating a much more balanced and healthier diet.

Fact

Humans eat roughly 200 types of plants, though scientist estimate that there are about 100,000 edible species on Earth – out of the 400,000 different species of plants.

If you decide to forage for your food do NOT eat anything you are not 100% sure on what it is. There are many tasty edible mushrooms out there that you may come across on your daily walk however there are just as many if not more that can be extremely dangerous if digested so my motto is "if you don't know it, throw it".

A great idea is to buy a small pocket foraging guide to carry with you when your out and about and you can use it if you're not quite sure. I've also added some "Note" pages to the back of this book so when you're out on your own cooking wild adventure, you can make notes of locations of wild edibles you come across, document wildlife or make note of idyllic spots to sit and enjoy future meals in the wilderness.

Whenever you decide to go the whole hog and not only eat but cook wild as well, the most important rule of them all is "leave no trace". It is so important that these beautiful wild and wonderful places stay that way for generations to come. Leaving burn marks in the ground from your campfire, litter in the hedge bottoms or even big areas that you've trampled down will only cause damage to that area and all the wildlife that lives there, so not only do you need to leave it exactly how it was when you arrived but try to safely take at least one bit of extra litter home with you too.

"Take only memories, leave only footprints."
— Chief Seattle.

Contents

Brunch

- 18. BBQ beans with fried egg on toast
- 20. Blueberry pancakes and bacon with the kids at the bottom of the garden.
- 22. Avocado and smoked salmon
- 24. Breakfast potatoes with chorizo & poached egg
- 26. Wild mushrooms with savoy cabbage.
- 28. Bubble and squeak with pan roasted vine tomatoes.

Fish

- 32. Seafood chowder on the beach.
- 34. Whole baked trout in a loch.
- 36. Pan fried sea bass on the coast.
- 38. Fish and chips by the sea.
- 40. Garlic Prawns sizzle dish.
- 42. Whitebait with garlic mayonnaise.

Vegetarian

- 46. Vegetable curry summit style.
- 48. Farmhouse vegetable soup.
- 50. Courgette and pesto pasta.
- 52. Nature's salad in a meadow.
- 54. Savoy stir fry with nuts and berries.
- 56. Spinach pancakes.

Meat

- 60. Beef and venison hotpot on a Scottish Munro.
- 62. Steak in the woods.
- 64. Game pie on the farm.
- 66. Spatchcock chicken and streaky bacon club sandwich in woods.
- 68. Jerk pork with stuffing and a sweetcorn fritter.
- 70. Lamb cutlets with Basmati rice and curried mayonnaise.

Small Dishes

- 74. Game goujons
- 75. Chargrilled vegetables
- 76. Sweet potato wedges
- 77. Onion rings in bitter batter.
- 78. Damper bread.
- 79. Bruschetta with mozzarella.

Sweet

- 82. Smoors by the campfire.
- 84. "Grown up's" Fire baked chocolate bananas.
- 86. Biscoff popcorn pudding jar.
- 88. Mum's flapjacks.

Drinks

- 92. Pine needle tea.
- 94. Ginger and spiced apple tea.
- 96. Mountaineers' hot chocolate.
- 98. Summer fruits mocktail.
- 100. Sloe Gin.
- 102. Pineapple and rum cocktail.

Extra bits

- 108. BBQ
- 109. Basic Bushcraft
- 111. Kit List.
- 112. Outdoors vs Epilepsy.
- 116. Peak District Walk.
- 122. Bonus Recipes.
- 124. Guide to seasonal fruit and vegetables.
- 127. Acknowledgements.
- 129. About the illustrator.

Brunch

"Cooking and eating food outdoors makes it taste infinitely better than the same meal prepared and consumed indoors."

– Fennel Hudson

BBQ beans with fried egg on toast

Ingredients

1 tin of baked beans.
Squeeze of bbq sauce.
Splash of tobasco.
Black pepper.
1 large free-range egg.
Splash of oil.

1 large slice of crusty loaf.
Small handful of flatleaf parsley.

Prep

This is best cooked on an open fire so make your campfire and get it going, it's ready to use one the flames have died down. Open the tin of beans but don't fully remove the lid. Add to the beans a good squeeze of bbq sauce, a splash of tabasco and a good grind of pepper. You can use the tin lid as a cover whilst cooking or keeping it warm. Roughly chop the parsley.

Method

Place the tin of beans on the edge of the fire and turn occasionally as well as the odd stir. Put the slice of bread into a non-stick pan and slowly toast on the fire. Once your toast is done put it on your plate and leave to one side. Now add a splash of oil to the pan and gently fry the egg. It's important that the pan isn't too hot, or it will just burn. Once the beans are starting to bubble they are ready, so remove from the fire and pour over the toast. Add your fried egg on top along with a grind of pepper and sprig of parsley.

" What better way to start the day than a warm, hearty, rustic breakfast sat by a camp fire listening to the morning sounds of the woodland."

Blueberry pancakes with bacon
With the kids at the bottom of the garden

Ingredients

One pack of American style Pancakes.
6 to 10 rashers of streaky maple bacon.
1 cup of blueberries.
A few generous tablespoons of golden or maple syrup.
1 tablespoon of icing sugar.

Prep

You can make your own pancakes if you want to, but this child-friendly meal is easier and quicker if you just to buy a pack.

Method

In a non-stick pan fry off your streaky bacon. You shouldn't need any oil or butter to cook in as bacon will release its own fat while cooking. Once cooked take out the pan and rest on some kitchen roll. Now simply add as many pancakes into the pan that will fit and warm them through, remembering to turn them over warming both sides. Grab a plate, add a drop of syrup to the centre of it and put your first pancake onto it, this just helps stop them sliding around. Layer them up by adding pancake, bacon, blueberries, syrup to each layer. When you get to the top pancake drizzle the remaining syrup over it, scatter with more blueberries and then dust with icing sugar.

" Make sure that campfires lit, and all the kids have got their spoons before digging into that sweet, sticky stack of heaven. There will be plenty of energy afterwards for campfire songs and games."

Smoked salmon with avocado

Ingredients

1 ripe avocado.
2 slices of smoked salmon.
1 fillet of hot smoked salmon.
Black pepper.
1 wedge of fresh lemon.
Dash of Worcester sauce.

Prep

Slice the avocado in half and remove the large stone. Scoop out the avocado and place on a board. Roughly dice the avocado and slices of smoked salmon and place into a bowl, season with a grind of pepper and a splash of Worcester sauce. Carefully remove the skin from the salmon fillet.

Method

All that's left to do is plate up! I like to spoon the avocado mix down the centre of the plate and then place the salmon fillet ontop. Finish it off with a squeeze of fresh lemon juice.

" This is such a simple dish, yet packed full of healthy fats and oils, perfect for the day ahead. "

Breakfast potatoes with chorizo and poached egg

Ingredients

1 large fresh free-range egg.
Roughly 80 - 100g of diced chorizo.
1 large handful of new potatoes.
1 teaspoon of paprika.
1 tablespoon of breadcrumbs.
Salt.

Pepper.
Few sprigs of flat leaf parsley.

Prep

Slice the potatoes in half or quarters depending on how big they are, bite-size is ideal. Roughly chop your flat leaf parsley. Crack the egg into a small dish.

Method

Place your potatoes in a saucepan and cover with cold water. Bring the pan to the boil and then simmer for 6 - 8 mins until cooked but still firm, drain and put to one side. Using the same saucepan, add enough cold water to cover the bottom with 3 – 4 inches of water then bring it to the boil. While that's coming to the boil heat up a non-stick pan and add your diced chorizo, potatoes, and breadcrumbs (you shouldn't need any oil as the natural oils will release from the chorizo) season with salt, pepper and paprika. Keep on the heat with the occasional toss or stir until they have become slightly crispy, then tip out onto some kitchen roll to absorb any excess oil. Now it's time for the egg. Turn off the gas or remove from the heat and carefully tip the egg into the hot water, after 3 mins gently remove the egg. Using a warm plate or bowl add your potatoes followed by your poached egg on top, then garnish by sprinkling on your parsley.

"Watch how satisfying it is, when you take that first cut into the egg and that lovely runny yolk oozes down trough the potatoes and chorizo."

Wild Mushrooms On toast

Advice from a Mushroom

Be down-to-earth

Sprout new ideas

Keep a low profile

Know when to show up

Stay well-rounded

Start from the ground up

Be a fun-guy!

Ingredients

2 slices sourdough bread.
Good nub of unsalted butter.
Drizzle of extra virgin olive oil.
2 handfuls (per person) of seasonal wild mushrooms.
Good splash of double cream.

bunch of chives.
bunch of parsley.
couple of wild garlic leaves.
salt and pepper.

Prep

Gently chop the wild garlic. Roughly chop the parsley and chives

Method

Cook the sourdough on a hot dry griddle for that charred flavour, I prefer the taste, and the scorch lines add to the presentation.

In a frying pan, heat a splash of oil and a good nub of butter. Add the mushrooms and chopped garlic.

Fry over a high heat until just cooked. Add the double cream and cook until the volume of liquid has reduced, and the mushrooms are glazed and creamy. Add in the chives, parsley and a twist of salt and pepper to taste.

Serve the mushrooms on the toast with an extra drizzle of olive oil.

"What an earthy way start the day. With the wild mushrooms and fresh garlic, you can almost taste the woodland. If your feeling like adding something special to this dish then swap your final drizzle of olive oil for the more expensive truffle oil."

Bubble and Squeak with fried duck egg and pan roasted vine tomatoes

Ingredients

Leftovers from the previous days roast dinner. Whatever you have you can use it in this dish!

Potatoes.

Cooked meat.

Vegetables.

Vine cherry tomatoes, left on the vine.

1 free range duck egg.

Fresh flatleaf parsley.

Olive oil.

Unsalted butter.

Prep

All you really need to do with this dish is to have enough potatoes to bind the ingredients together, so if you don't have enough left over, then peel boil and mash enough potatoes for the amount of people you're serving. Dice all the leftover ingredients into bitesize pieces and add to the mashed potatoes in a mixing bowl. Add a good grind of pepper and salt, a splash of olive oil and some chopped parsley. Fold all the ingredients together.

Method

Using a large non-stick pan, add a splash of olive oil and a small nub of butter, heat to a medium temperature and then add you mix. Flatten the mixture out over the pan and turn the heat down low. After roughly 5 minutes turn the mixture over and cook for a further 5 minutes, you're looking for a slightly golden crispy finish on the top and bottom. Once this is achieved place to one side and cover with foil or place in the oven to keep warm. You now add your tomatoes still on the vine to a pan, drizzle with olive oil, a grind of pepper and a nub of butter and cook gently without tuning them but baste them if you can. Using a non-stick pan, fry your duck egg in oil being carful not to burn the white or break the yolk, the key to this is not to get the pan too hot!

Time to serve. Take the pan of bubble and squeak and carefully tip it upside down onto a serving plate. Add the roasted tomatoes to the side and place the egg on top!

" *Use a big spoon to serve, and watch that beautiful rich and runny yolk ooze down into the bubble and squeak, adding to that comforting flavour.* "

Fish

Seafood chowder
on the beach

Ingredients

- 4 big glugs of white wine.
- 1 glug of olive oil.
- 1 large nub of unsalted butter.
- 4 tablespoons of double cream.
- 1 lemon.
- 1 small handful of parsley.
- Black pepper.
- 6 garlic cloves.
- 1 red chilli.
- 1/2 a white onion.
- 2 fillets of white fish (cod/haddock/pollock).
- 2 crab's claws.
- 1 Large handful of mussels.
- 1 handful of prawns.
- 1 fillet of salmon.
- 1 small handful of baby potatoes.
- 1 small handful of samphire grass.

Prep

Cut your baby potatoes in half and dice your white fish and salmon into chunks roughly the same size as your potatoes. Peel and finely chop the onion.

Clean your mussels in clean water by removing any beards and grit, throwing away any that are already open.

Slice the chilli into small rings, discarding of the seeds. Roughly chop the parsley.

Method

Place one medium pan on the gas hob adding the butter, olive oil and chopped onion and sauté gently for a couple of mins. Add your potatoes and cover with cold water, bring to the boil then simmer for five mins.

Add your garlic, followed by your crabs' claws, salmon, white fish, mussels, good glug of white wine and the juice of half a lemon into the pan. Close the lid and leave for 2-3 mins.

Now add the prawns, the samphire grass, chilli and parsley, along with a good few turns of the pepper mill. Stir the pan delicately a couple of times taking care not to break up the fish. Close the lid and leave for a further 3-4 mins on a medium heat until its piping hot.

" Serve into two bowls with some lovely rustic bread to mop up the juices and a glass of your favourite white wine."

" Watch me cook this on YouTube "

Channel: Wildernessrobbo | **Play list:** Cooking in the wild
Video: Seafood Chowder

Whole Baked Rainbow Trout
With sweet potato wedges and asparagus
In a loch

Ingredients

1 whole rainbow trout.
1 medium sweet potato.
6 fresh asparagus.
1 whole lemon.
Smoked sea salt.
Glug of white wine.

Pepper.
Flat leaf parsley.
Unsalted butter.
Extra virgin Olive oil.
Tin foil.

Prep

Gut and clean your trout if it's freshly caught with cold water. Rinse off the sweet potatoes and slice into rough wedges. Slice the lemon in half.

Method

Season the inside of the trout with some sea salt and pepper, adding four slices of lemon, a couple of nubs of butter and a bunch of parsley. Season the outside with more salt and pepper. Leave to one side. Put a pan on a medium to high heat with a drizzle of olive oil and add your sweet potato wedges, season well and toss ensuring they don't stick. Turn down the heat and cover with some foil or place in the centre of the oven on a medium heat. Ensuring you use a good non-stick pan, add a nub of butter a drizzle of olive oil and place in your fish on low to medium heat. Leave cooking for up to 5 mins then gently turn over add a good glug of white wine and cover with foil. Leave for another 5 minutes and then take off the heat but leave covered with foil. If you have a griddle pan for your asparagus, then use that if not a normal pan it fine. Place in your asparagus on a medium heat season with pepper and ad a nub of butter and toss over for a few mins until cooked al dente. Now its time to plate up! Using an oval plate, place your trout to one edge with your sweet potato wedges and asparagus opposite.

"Squeeze a little lemon over the fish and serve with a large glass of white wine ensuring you keep one eye open for the loch ness monster as you tuck in."

" Watch me cook this on YouTube "

Channel: Wildernessrobbo | **Play list:** Cooking in the wild
Video: Trout Recipe done Loch side

Pan Fried Sea Bass

With pak choi and balsamic vine tomatoes

On the coast

Ingredients

2 fillets of sea bass.
Small handful of baby potatoes.
1 whole pak choi.
6 on the vine cherry tomatoes.
Unsalted Butter.

Black pepper.
Few sprigs of flat leaf parsley.
Balsamic vinegar.
Olive oil.

Prep

Slice the pak choi in half and cut out the main stem at the bottom which can be discarded. Cut the baby potatoes in half and place in some cold water.

Method

Season your pan of water with salt and pepper and bring your potatoes to the boil, then simmer for roughly 10 minutes until the potatoes are soft enough to eat. Drain the water, add a small nub of butter, cover and leave them to one side. Using a griddle pan, if you have one, place the pak choi flat side down along with a nub of butter onto the hot griddle to create scorch lines on them. Turn them over reduce the heat and leave to cook further. In a small pan, add a nub of butter and a splash of olive oil, turn on the heat and add your vine of cherry tomatoes. Now season with salt, pepper and a good splash of balsamic vinegar. Cover with tin foil and roast gently in the oven for up to 10 minutes. Using a non-stick pan add a splash of olive oil and a nub of butter and put onto a gentle heat. Place your two fillets of sea bass skin side down into the pan. As you do, gently move the fish with your fingertips. This ensures it doesn't stick as you place it down, as well as stopping the ends from curling up at the edges. Cook for roughly 2 minutes before gently tuning the fish with a spatula and cooking for a further 2 minutes. Time to plate up! Take your new potatoes, season with salt and pepper then start gently crushing them with a masher or fork (just enough to crush them, you're not looking to mash the potatoes), place them slightly off-centre or your plate alongside your crossed over pak choi and the vine of roasted tomatoes. Place your beautiful Sea Bass cris crossed over your potatoes. Sprinkle with some flat leaf parsley and drizzle some of the leftover reduction from your balsamic tomatoes, and there you have it, your own slice of the Mediterranean! Sea bass with crushed potatoes, pak choi and balsamic tomatoes.

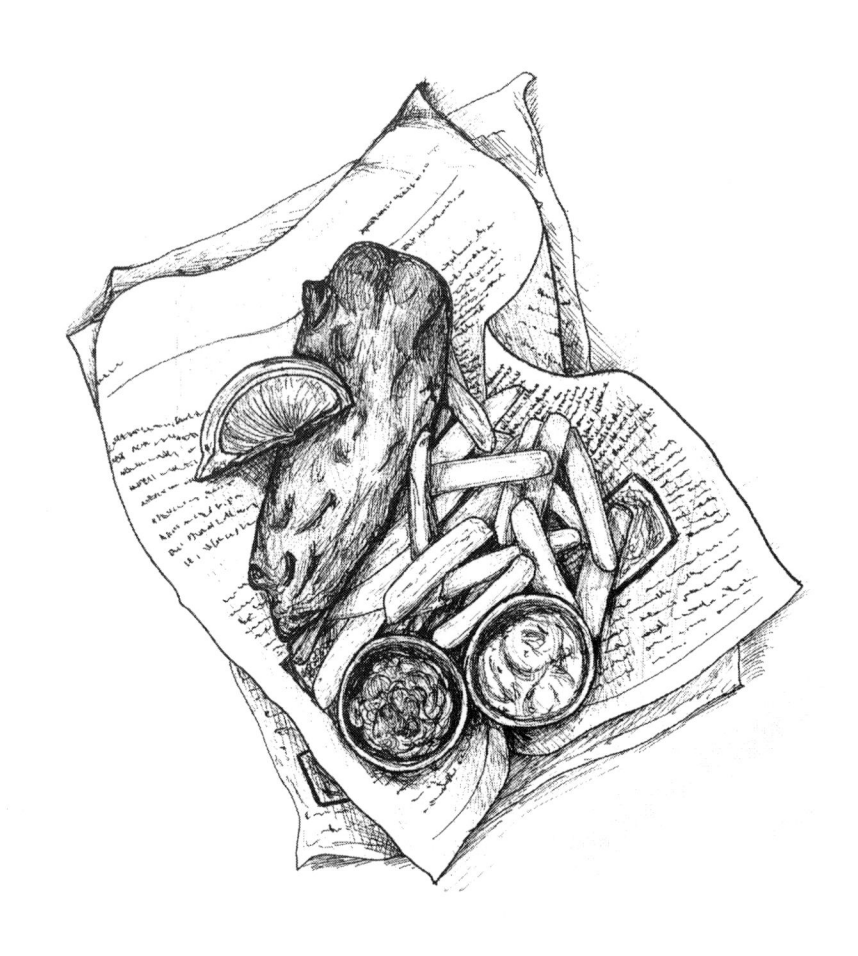

Fish and Chips
With mushy peas
By the sea

Ingredients

1 cod/haddock fillet.
Potato.
1 small tin of mushy peas.
Few sprigs of mint.
1 lemon.
Butter.

1 ½ cups of plain flour.
1 bottle of beer or real ale.
Sea Salt.
Vegetable Oil.
Vinegar.

Prep

Take your potatoes and cut into chunky, wedge-style chips, leaving the skin on and try to get them all a similar size, so they cook at the same time. To one side put your peas into a small saucepan. Finely chop your mint and add to the peas, along with some pepper, a nub of butter and a splash of vinegar. In a large bowl put 1 cup of flour along with a good pinch of salt. Form a well in the middle and slowly pour in the beer/ale whisking constantly until smooth and light. Put the remaining half a cup of flour onto a plate to dip the fish in later.

Method

Put your vegetable oil into a large saucepan and bring up to temperature. You can test this by putting in one small chip if there is a moderate sizzle then your good to go. However if there is no sizzle it's not hot enough and if there is excessive sizzle and splatter its too hot. Now you have the ideal heat, add all of your potatoes gently to the oil and cook until soft and golden brown. While your chips are cooking, coat your fish in the flour on the plate. Put your peas on a low heat stirring occasionally. Put down some kitchen roll and place the cooked chips onto them to drain any excess oil off, placing another piece of kitchen roll on top. Dip your fish into the batter ensuring its covered completely. Using the same oil as the chips had been in bring back to the correct heat and place your fish into the oil until the batter is golden brown. Once cooked, scoop out and place on some kitchen roll to drain. Serve the chips, beer battered fish and mushy peas with some flakes of sea salt and a good wedge of fresh lemon.

"Now sit and enjoy listening to the seagulls and crash of the waves."

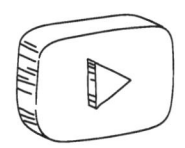

" Watch me cook this on YouTube "

Channel: Wildernessrobbo | **Play list:** Cooking in the wild
Video: Beer battered Fish and Chips

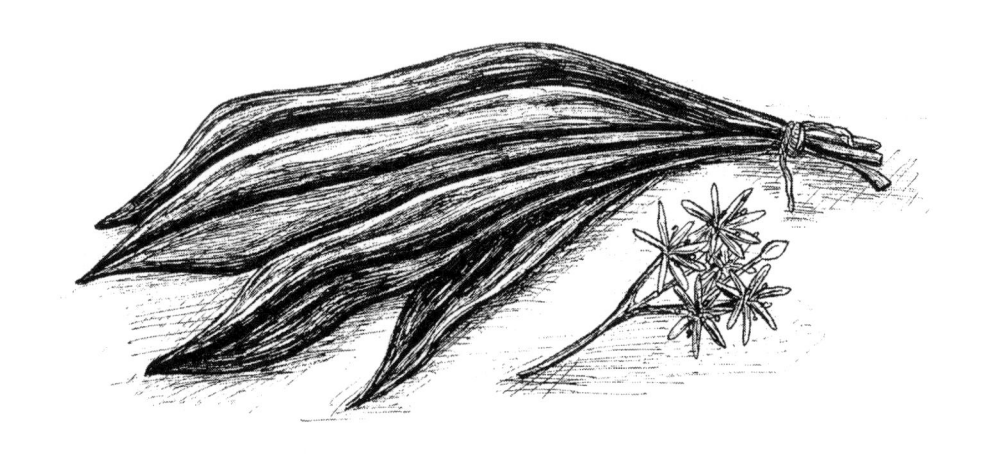

Garlic Prawns Sizzle Dish

Ingredients

6 – 8 raw peeled and prepped king prawn (per person).
1 bulb of fresh garlic.
Small handful of wild garlic leaves.
1 garlic flower head.
Half a block of unsalted butter.
Glug of white wine.

Black pepper.
Good glug of extra virgin olive oil.
Small handful of flatleaf parsley.
Half a lemon.
Handful of fresh young salad.
Few slices of hard rustic crusty bread.

Prep

You will need an individual oven proof dish for this recipe the size of a small side plate/dish. First job is to slice your garlic in half, so you have a top and a bottom. Put the bottom half to one side and using the cloves from the top half, thinly slice. Finely chop your wild garlic leaves and flatleaf parsley. Rinse your garlic flower head and leave on a bit of kitchen roll to dry. De-vein the prawns if required.

Method

Place the bottom of your garlic bulb in your small dish, drizzle with a little olive oil and place in a hot oven or closed lid BBQ to roast. Prep your salad by putting your leaves in a bowl, pick the petal heads from the garlic flower and add those as well as a squeeze of fresh lemon. Get a dry griddle pan nice and hot and toast the slices of bread creating some lovely scorch lines. In a pan, add a good glug of extra virgin olive oil and the butter, melt down but be careful not to burn! Once the butter has meted and reached temperature add directly one after the other the thinly sliced garlic, the glug of white wine, the chopped parsley and wild garlic, the prawns, a grind of black pepper and a squeeze of lemon. You need to cook the prawns until they have turned a lovely orange/pink colour, this will only take a few minutes, now take off the heat. To serve I like to use a cold white square plate. Take out your dish with the garlic bulb from the oven and place on the plate to one corner. Put the garlic bulb at the side of the dish and add the toast and a handful of salad. Now carefully spoon the prawns and as much as the garlic butter into the hot dish as you want, make sure there is enough to dip that rustic bread into as I promise you, the taste is both heavenly and indulgent!

Devilled Whitebait

Ingredients

- 50g cornflour.
- 50g plain flour.
- 2 tbsp sweet smoked paprika.
- 2 tsp cayenne pepper.
- 200g fresh or frozen whitebait (if frozen, defrost thoroughly).
- Vegetable oil.
- 4 cloves garlic.
- 1 tbsp olive oil.
- Good pinch of flaked sea salt.
- 5 tbsp mayonnaise (good quality shop bought is fine, or you can make your own).
- 1 wedge of lemon.
- Small sprig of fresh dill.

Prep

Put the cornflour, Plain flour, paprika and cayenne into a bowl and mix well. Add the whitebait and toss well, until covered in the spiced flour. Roughly chop the dill.

Method

To start with, put the garlic cloves onto a piece of foil, drizzle with the olive oil, sprinkle with sea salt and wrap up tightly. Roast for roughly 25-30 minutes until soft. Cool, then squeeze the cloves out of their skins and put in a bowl with the mayonnaise, add a small drizzle of olive oil and mix well. Finish off with a sprinkle of sea salt, dill, paprika and a lemon wedge to squeeze over.

Fill a saucepan roughly 1/3 full with veg oil and heat up until a cube of bread browns in 30 seconds. Fry the whitebait, in batches, for 4-5 minutes or until lovely and crisp. Drain on greaseproof paper and keep warm in a low oven while you fry the rest. I like to serve in a basket with the roasted garlic mayonnaise for dipping. Finish off with a sprinkle of sea salt, paprika and lemon wedge to squeeze over.

" This can be served as a starter or a main, just adjust the quantities accordingly. Either way it's a fish dish that's a firm favourite in our family. "

Vegetarian

Vegetable Curry

Summit style

Ingredients

- 1 tbsp of olive oil.
- 1 small onion.
- 2 garlic cloves.
- 1 tbsp grated fresh ginger.
- 1 tbsp of medium curry powder.
- 2 tsp of cumin powder.
- 6 cardamon pods.
- 1 small chilli.
- 400g tin light coconut milk.
- 1 small cauliflower.
- 400g tin chickpeas.
- 1 lemon.
- Handful of flatleaf parsley.
- 1 naan bread.

Prep

Peel and slice the onion. Cut the cauliflower into medium sized florets and trim the stalks. Cut the lemon into wedges. Take a handful of the parsley (leaving a few sprigs to one side) and roughly chop. Slice the chilli in half, deseed it and finely chop the two halves separately. Finely chop or crush the garlic cloves.

Method

Heat the olive oil in a saucepan and fry the onion for roughly 5 minutes until softened. Add the garlic and ginger and fry for a couple of minutes, then stir in the curry, cumin and cardamon pods and cook for 30 seconds.

Add the coconut milk, cauliflower, the tin of chickpeas including the liquid and half of your chopped fresh chilli. Partially cover the pan and bring to the boil, then add the chopped parsley and simmer until the cauliflower is tender and the sauce has thickened. If the sauce reduces too much before the cauliflower is ready, splash in some water or a glug of white wine. Or, if the cauliflower is nearly done and the sauce is too thin, take the lid off to allow the sauce to reduce. Squeeze in some fresh lemon juice wedges to taste. The curry shouldn't need any salt. Grab your plate or shallow bowl, and scatter with the remaining chopped chilli if you like it hot. Garnish with the sprig of parsley a wedge of lemon and serve with naan bread.

" *Watch me cook this on YouTube* "

Channel: Wildernessrobbo | **Play list:** Cooking in the wild
Video: veg curry summit style

Vegetable Soup

Down on the farm

Ingredients

- 1 onion.
- 1 leek.
- 2 medium white potatoes.
- 2 carrots.
- 1 parsnip.
- 1 stick of celery.
- Fresh chives.
- Salt and pepper.
- Large nub of butter.
- Glug of olive oil.
- Teaspoon of paprika.
- Glug of double cream.
- Glass of white wine.
- 1 litre of vegetable stock.

Prep

Peel and finely chop the onion. Wash and roughly chop your leek and celery. Peel and dice your potatoes and carrots into large bite-size pieces. Roughly chop your fresh chives.

Method

You'll need to use a large saucepan that you have a lid for, however you can always use kitchen foil if you can't find a lid. Add a nub of butter and a glug of good quality olive oil to the pan and add your onion, followed by your leek. Keep the onion and leek moving so not to burn and stir fry for a minute or two. Add the potatoes and the glass of wine, now immediately turn down the heat. Pour in your veg stock and add the remaining carrots, parsnip and celery. Season with salt, pepper and paprika, stir well, place the lid on and gently simmer for 15 minutes. Remove the lid and pour in a good splash of double cream, stir well and give it a taste for any extra seasoning. Replace the lid and simmer for another 15 - 20 minutes before removing from the heat. If you want a thicker soup, then just cook for longer as it will reduce down over time. You can now blend the soup to make a smooth texture or even serve it as it is, the choice is yours and down to personal preference. My choice would be to leave it as it is, pour it into a thick ceramic bowl, sprinkle over the freshly-chopped chives, an extra grind of black pepper and some thickly sliced farmhouse granary bread.

" Find yourself a spot on the ground where you can lean against barn and watch the wildlife whilst enjoying all those big, hearty, warming flavours."

Courgette and pesto pasta

Ingredients

4 courgettes.
1 lemon.
1 lime.
Pine nuts.
Block of Parmesan cheese.
Bunch of fresh basil.

2 cloves of garlic.
Black pepper.
Extra virgin olive oil.
Large nub of butter.
Sun-dried tomatoes.

Prep

This dish is all in the prep, once that is done the cooking time is extremely short. To start with, make your pesto using either a pestle and mortar or small food blender. Add a handful of fresh basil leaves, 2 cloves of garlic, a tablespoon of pine nuts, a good glug of olive oil, a few twists of pepper and a teaspoon of parmesan gratings then blend it all together until you have a paste. You may want to add more olive oil to get a more liquid paste. Take your courgettes and cut off and discard of the ends. Using a sharp knife, slice length ways down the courgette, creating thin ribbons roughly 5mm thick. Once you have your ribbons, cut diagonally through them again across the width creating matchstick size pieces of courgette. In a large bowl, add your courgette, a handful of sun-dried tomatoes, a tablespoon of pine nuts, a good grind of pepper and using your fingers gently mix together.

Method

Using a non-stick pan, put on a medium heat with a small glug of olive oil and a good nub of butter. Now add your bowl of courgette ingredients to the heat and toss in the butter for roughly 5 minutes. Take off the heat and put back into the large bowl, this time adding your pesto along with a squeeze of fresh lemon and lime. Mix thoroughly with your fingers. Take a clean white bowl or plate and present your courgette in the same way you would spaghetti. Garnish with a few fresh basil leaves, some Parmesan shavings and a quick drizzle of olive oil.

"I would recommend a glass of good crisp white wine to go with this dish."

Natures Salad

in a meadow

Ingredients

Small handful of pansies (6).
Teaspoon of poppy seeds.
Tablespoon of sunflower seeds.
Small handful of viola's (6).
Dandelions (6).
2 fresh radishes.
Handful of wild garlic leaves.

Handful of fresh mint.
Handful of mixed salad leaf.
Teaspoon of wholegrain mustard.
Large glug of extra virgin olive oil.
Teaspoon of balsamic vinegar.
1 slice of rustic farmhouse loaf.

Note

Note: When picking wildflowers and plants always be 100% sure of what they are to ensure you don't pick a poisonous variety. You should only ever pick what you need, there is no point picking a bucket full if you're only going to use a handful and end up throwing the rest away.

Method

Start by roughly chopping up your garlic leaves and mint. Slice your radishes as thin as you can get them. In a bowl, place in your mixed salad leaves along with your garlic, mint and radishes. In a separate bowl, make a dressing using the whole grain mustard, olive oil and balsamic vinegar season with salt and pepper if required. Take your slice of rustic loaf and drizzle with a little olive oil and toast in a pan both sides until crispy. Remove from the heat and roughly cut into cubes to make croutons, adding them to the salad bowl. Now add the sunflower seeds, the heads and leaves of the dandelions, plus a drizzle of your dressing and gently mix together. Put your salad into your chosen bowl and garnish with the pansy and viola heads with a sprinkle of poppy seeds to finish.

" Now sit back in the meadow with the sun on your face a glass of iced lemon water or crisp white wine and enjoy a fresh healthy salad provided by mother nature."

Savoy stir fry
with nuts, seeds and berries

Ingredients

- 1x whole savoy cabbage.
- A small wedge of good blue cheese.
- Small handful of pomegranate seeds
- Small handful of flaked almonds.
- Small handful of plain unsalted cashew nuts.
- Small handful of walnuts.
- Small handful of sesame seeds.
- Large nub of unsalted butter.
- 1x tbsp of sesame oil.
- Small handful of dried cranberries.
- 1x large shallot.
- Handful of croutons.
- Salt and pepper.
- 1x tsp of paprika.
- 1x tsp cumin.
- ½ tsp of chilli flakes.
- Small handful of fresh coriander.

Prep

Remove and discard the stalk from the cabbage then roughly slice/shred the cabbage into strips. Peel and slice the shallot. Dice the dried cranberries into small pieces. Rinse and chop the coriander.

Method

In a dry pan, gently warm/toast the cashew nuts, walnuts, flaked almonds, sesame seeds and croutons, being very careful not to burn. Once done, leave in pan but remove from the heat. Heat up a wok and then add a good glug of sesame oil. Now add your shredded cabbage and shallot. Season with salt and pepper, add your nub of butter and toss. After a few minutes and the cabbage has begun to wilt add your paprika, cumin and chilli flakes and toss several times. After a few more minutes when the cabbage is cooked al dente remove from the heat. Add and mix in your cranberries and the warm seeds, nuts and croutons. Time to serve into a lovely rustic bowl and top off with the fresh pomegranate seeds, a crumble of blue cheese and a sprinkle of fresh coriander.

" This dish is extremely tasty and full of natural healthy ingredients perfect to enjoy on its own or as part of a bigger meal."

Spinach pancakes

Ingredients

1 cup of self-raising flour.
1 cup of semi skimmed milk.
1 free-range egg.
Black pepper.
100g of baby washed spinach.

Nub of unsalted butter.
Glug of olive oil.

Prep

Wilt the spinach briefly over some boiling water and then leave to cool in a sieve.

Method

Put the flour, milk, spinach, cracked egg and a few grinds of the pepper mill into a blender and blitz until smooth. Using a good non-stick frying pan, heat up a small amount of butter and oil then add a ladle of the mixture. Cook for a couple of minutes before flipping and cooking the other side.

" These are a great healthy savoury pancake that you can make large thin ones or smaller thicker ones which go really well with an avocado and poached egg salad or some grilled streaky bacon! "

Meat

Venison Hot Pot
On a Scottish Munro

Ingredients

250-400g of diced venison.
Two carrots.
1 red onion.
Sprig of sage.
Sprig of thyme.
1 bay leaf.
Large nub of butter.
A glug of Olive oil.

Bacon lardons.
1 tablespoon of plain flour.
Handful of chestnut mushrooms.
1 bottle of dark ale.
1 – 2 large white potatoes.
1 teaspoon of whole grain mustard.
Cup of beef stock.

Prep

Peel and thinly slice your potatoes, they don't need to be a perfect shape but try to get them all roughly the same thickness, this helps them cook evenly. Clean your carrots (I prefer not to peel them) and roughly dice. Peel and finely chop the red onion. If the chestnut mushrooms are large then half or quarter them, however, feel free to leave them whole.

Method

Bring a pan to heat with a glug of olive oil and add your carrot, red onion and lardons. Follow with your diced venison and mix together, now turn down the heat. Add your flour followed by the beef stock, nub of butter, whole grain mustard, thyme, sage and bay leaf. Now pour in your chosen bottle of dark ale, ensuring you sample a taste first to make sure it tastes good! Stir well and leave on a very low heat for 5 – 10 minutes.

Depending on how you're cooking the next stage of this depends on the dish/pot you use, but transfer all your ingredients from the pan into a pot making sure you don't leave any juice behind. Thinly cover the top with your sliced potatoes, sprinkle on a little salt n pepper, cover with a lid and cook low and slow for around a couple of hours removing the lid 10 minutes before the end to crisp up your potatoes.

" What better place to enjoy this hearty warming meal accompanied by a glass of your favourite red than finding a sheltered spot on the summit of a beautiful and majestic Scottish Munro looking out across the land that the regal deer roams wild and free."

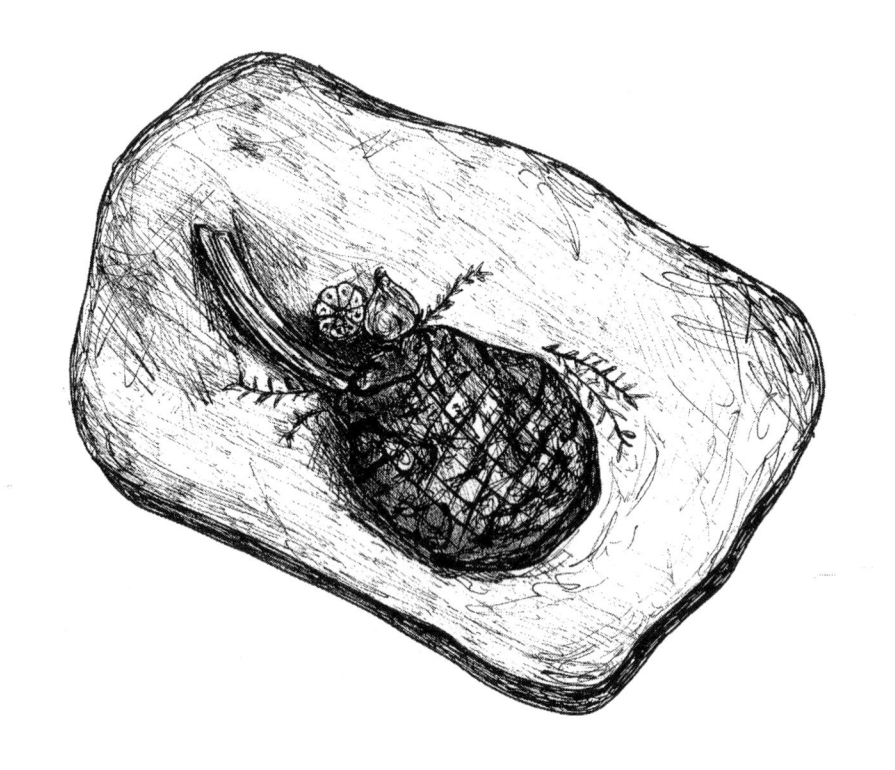

Cowboy Steak
In the woods

" *Watch me cook this on YouTube* "

Channel: Wildernessrobbo | **Play list:** Cooking in the wild
Video: Tomahawk steak in the woods

Ingredients

1 tomahawk (cowboy) steak.
1 large or 2 medium field mushrooms.
1 whole garlic bulb.
Smoked sea salt.
Black pepper.
Bunch of fresh thyme.
Bunch of flatleaf parsley.

Gorse flowers.
Half a block of unsalted butter.
Glug of extra virgin olive oil.
Teaspoon of paprika.
Teaspoon of cumin.
Teaspoon of chilli flakes.

Prep

First of all, you need to make your rub. To do this take a pestle and mortar and mix together the chilli flakes, paprika, cumin, salt, pepper and the leaves from 2-3 sprigs of thyme. Mix the ingredients together and rub all over the steak and then leave to one side. Tie the remainder of the thyme up at one end to use as a basting brush later. Cut you garlic bulb in half leaving all its skin on. Roughly chop a few sprigs of parsley and place into a small dish with your butter allowing it to soften enough that you will be able to brush it on with your thyme. Ideally your steak should be cooked on a wire grid or griddle over an open flame to really take on the flame-grilled smoky taste, so if cooking outside it's time to light your campfire or BBQ.

Method

Once you have the desired heat, when it comes to steak, I prefer hotter the better, place your steak onto the grid and sear it for a minute or two both sides. Now begin to cook this should take roughly 15 minutes each side, however you need to take into consideration the size and thickness of the cut, how hot the cooking temperature is ,and most importantly, if you like your meat rare, medium rare, or dare I say it, well done! Make sure you baste your steak regularly, using your thyme dipped in butter to keep that meat moist and juicy. Once you have started the cooking of your steak drizzle some olive oil over the cut end of the garlic and add to the griddle to bake. With roughly 10 minutes of cooking time left, add some of your basting butter along with a splash of olive oil to your mushrooms and add them to the griddle as well. Once you have cooked the steak to your liking remove from the heat and leave to rest for 5 minutes. Its now time to plate up.

"I like to serve my tomahawk steak with field mushroom and roasted garlic on a thick, rustic chopping board and garnish it with a sprinkling of fresh gorse flowers and wash it down with a quality real ale."

Game Pie
From field to fork

Ingredients

Partridge breast.
Pheasant breast.
Pigeon breast.
1 large potato.
2 carrots.
Beef stock.
French beans.

1 teaspoon of wholegrain mustard.
Glug of red wine.
Glug of olive oil.
2 shallots.
Tablespoon of plain flour.
Salt and pepper.
Puff pastry sheet.

Prep

Peel and chop your carrots and potato into small cubes. Slice your partridge, pheasant and pigeon into small strips and gently flour. Peel your shallots and quarter. Trim your French beans if required. Using a sheet of shop-bought puff pastry (you can make it yourself, but there really is no need) use a round object roughly 12cm in diameter as a guide and cut out a circle. This will be the lid for your pie, so if you're doing 4 portions, you'll need 4 lids. Place the circles onto a tray that has been lined with baking paper and then glaze the lids with a little melted butter and a sprinkle of flaked sea salt.

Method

Using a saucepan on a medium heat, add a nub of butter, a glug of olive oil, followed by the carrots, potato, shallots and game. Season well with salt and pepper then add a large glug of good quality red wine and your beef stock, along with the mustard. You can use a tablespoon of plain flour to thicken your stock as it reduces. Turn the heat right down and simmer gently for at least 1 hour, stirring occasionally. Basically, you want to cook the meat until it is soft, juicy and tender, so don't be afraid to take a bit out and cook to your taste. Once your meat is to your liking you can simply turn off the heat but leave covered with the lid. Boil some water in another pan, season with pepper, add your French beans and simmer for roughly 5 – 7 minutes, but again don't be afraid to take one out to check its cooked to your correct texture before taking off the heat and draining. Whilst your beans are cooking put your puff pastry lid/lids into a hot oven for a few minutes until puffed up and golden in colour. Be sure to keep an eye on them as they can quickly go from golden to garbage in no time at all. Get a large shallow bowl and serve yourself a big ladle full of the game filling. Serve the beans to the side and top the filling off with your lovely crunchy golden puff pastry lid.

" Find your favourite spot on the shoot and appreciate the whole field to fork experience."

Spatchcock Chicken Club Sandwich
In the woods

Ingredients

- 1 whole chicken.
- Baby gem lettuce.
- 6 slices of Parma ham.
- Fresh large tomato.
- A large dollop of your favourite mayonnaise.
- Olive oil.
- Jerk seasoning.
- Salt and pepper.
- Bread of your choice - needs to be substantial like a thick farmhouse or ciabatta.

Prep

The first thing you need to do is start cooking your chicken, however you'll need to spatchcock it first. Take your chicken and place breast side down on a chopping board with the 'bum' of the bird pointing towards your tummy. Take a large pair of kitchen scissors and cut up one side of its backbone, then repeat the other side of the backbone. You should now be left with the backbone totally separate that you can throw away or use for stock on another dish. Turn the chicken back over and using the palm of your hands push down on it to flatten the bird out, creating a spatchcock chicken. I recommend using two metal skewers and poking them diagonally across the chicken creating a cross, this will help stop the chicken curling back up. Season your chicken with salt, pepper, jerk seasoning and olive oil. Now its time to BBQ it or oven roast if you can't.

Method

Cooking times will vary depending on the temperature, size of the chicken and the cooking method, but make sure it's piping hot and the juices run clear when you test it. I recommend testing after from 40 minutes with a spatchcock chicken. Once cooked leave on the side to rest and cool while you complete the rest of the sandwich. Tear off a few lettuce leaves and rinse with cold water. Slice your tomato into suitable sizes. Place your Parma ham on a hot griddle and cook with no oil or butter until lovely and crispy. Now take your bread and lightly toast 3 pieces, spreading your toast with a good dollop of mayonnaise and a grind of pepper. Here comes the fun part – fill two layers of your sandwich with a combination of warm chicken grilled Parma ham, lettuce and tomato, then top off with your final slice of toast before cutting in half and diving in to a simple yet gourmet sandwich with plenty of chicken left over for seconds!

Jerk pork and sweetcorn fritter with mango relish

Home-made Jerk Marinade

1 sweet red pepper.
5 sprigs of fresh thyme.
2 teaspoon salt.
1/2 teaspoon black pepper.
1 tablespoon brown sugar.
2 teaspoon ground allspice.
1 teaspoon nutmeg.
1 teaspoon cinnamon.

2 scotch bonnet peppers.
1/3 cup soy sauce.
2 tablespoon vegetable oil.
1/4 cup vinegar.
2 spring onions.
1/2 cup orange juice.
2 cloves garlic.
1 teaspoon grated ginger.

Basically, all you do is give everything a rough chop and place in a food processor or blender and pulse until you get a smooth consistency.

Ingredients

2 bottles or roughly 500 – 600g of jerk sauce (follow the recipe below to make your own).
1x Responsibly-sourced pork shoulder joint, roughly 2kg will serve 6 – 10 people.
1 - 2 corn on the cob.
Batter mix – 3 free range eggs, 30ml milk, 75g plain flour.

1 – 2 whole mangos.
Good squeeze of honey.
Unsalted butter.
Glug of olive oil.
1x lime.
1x red chilli.
6 – 12 brioche rolls.

Prep

Carefully remove the outer rind from the pork if it's still on and carefully score the remaining fat. Put your pork joint into a tray and cover with the marinade, ensuring it gets in all the nooks and crannies. Cover with cling film refrigerate for a minimum of 1 hr, however I like to do this the night before and marinade overnight. Cook your corn on a grill with a little butter then leave to cool before cutting off the sweetcorn. Make the batter by mixing the eggs, flour, milk together to get the right consistency and then add into the mix your sweetcorn, cover and leave to one side. Carefully peel and finely dice the mango, remembering there is a stone in the middle. Finley chop the chilli removing the seeds. Mix the diced mango, chilly, honey and juice of the lime into a bowl and leave covered.

Method

The best way to cook your pork for a truly authentic jerk taste is to BBQ it. I like to spit roast mine over hot coals. Try to keep the coals to one side and not directly underneath, this will help reduce the pork from getting burnt from any flames caused by dripping fat. I can't tell you how long to cook it for over the coals as it can vary due to many factors, however I recommend using a meat probe and ensure the inner temperature is a minimum of 145 degrees Fahrenheit or 65 degrees Celsius. Once cooked remove from the coals place on a board, cover with foil and leave to rest.
In a non stick pan add a dash of olive oil and nub of butter. Bring to a gentle heat and add a small ladle of your sweetcorn batter flipping to cook each side, repeat the process to cook all the mixture. Gently griddle the brioche buns to form some nice scorch lines.

Time to serve! Carve the pork, then load up your rolls with a combination of pork, sweetcorn fritter and a dollop of fresh mango.

"These are a fantastically tasty summer BBQ food that is great accompanied by a cool larger and lots of friends and family."

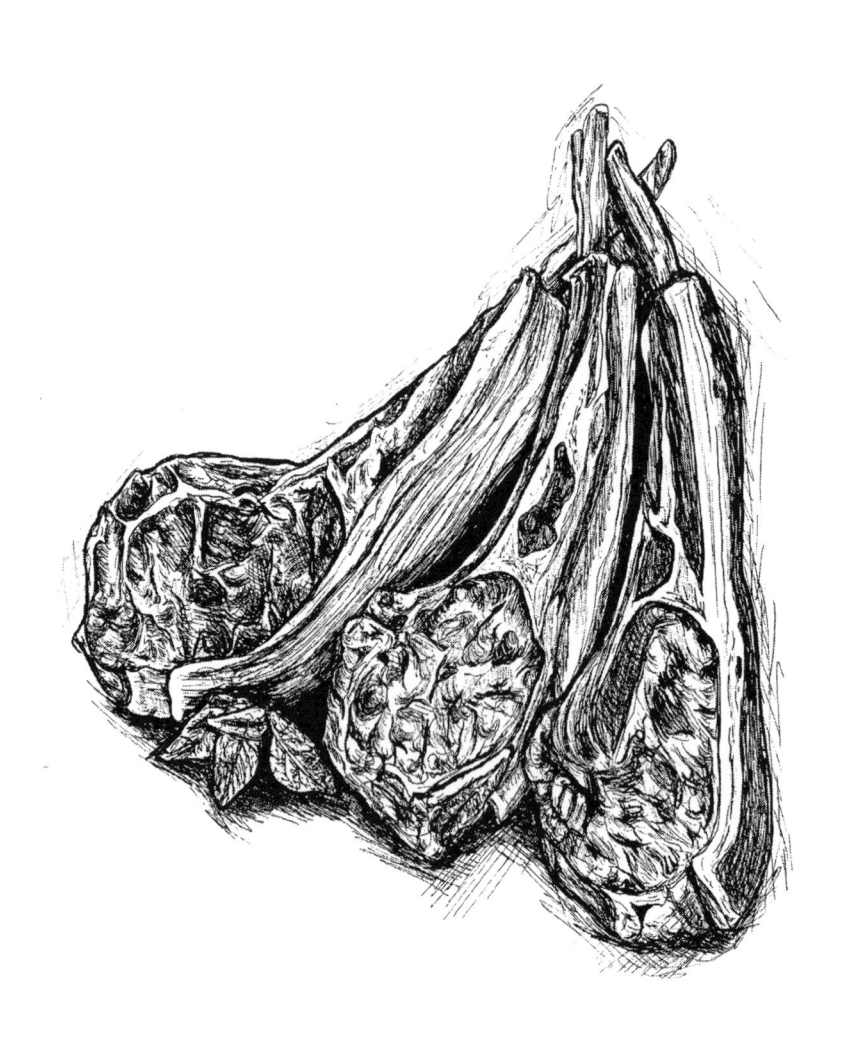

Lamb cutlets with Basmati rice and curried mayonnaise

Ingredients

3 farm-assured lamb cutlets per person.
1 cup of basmati rice.
Fresh coriander.
3 to 4 spoonfulls of good quality mayonnaise.

Small teaspoon of curry powder.
Good nub of unsalted butter.

Prep

Trim up any excess fat from the bone end of the cutlets leaving it nice and clean. Roughly chop your fresh coriander. Make your mayonnaise by simply adding a small splash of olive oil to the mayonnaise along with the dash of curry powder, fine tune it to your taste!

Method

Put the cup of rice into a pan and then add 2 cups of boiling water, now place on the heat and simmer for 7 minutes with no lid on. After 7 minutes remove from the heat add a good nub of butter, a twist of black pepper, cover with a lid and leave to one side. get a griddle pan hot and place the cutlets down, no oil should be needed as natural fats will release from the lamb. After around 3 minutes turn the cutlets over, achieving some nice char lines whilst cooking. Finish off by holding the cutlets on there side fat side down to ensure any fat is rendered down and crispy. Now remove from the pan and allow to rest while you serve the rice. Take the lid off the rice, add the chopped coriander and give it a stir to flake it up. You can either spoon your rice on or use a small mould or dish to fill and then turn upside down on your plate for better presentation. Lay the lamb cutlets on their end around the rice and add a good dollop of the curried mayonnaise to one side to dip the lamb into.

" This is a fantastic dish served outside in the summer griddling the lamb on the BBQ, or inside as a winter warmer. Possibly add a couple of poppadom's to dip in that mayonnaise."

Small Dishes

Game Goujons

Ingredients

Roughly 400g of your own choice of mixed game. I usually use a mixture of pheasant, partridge and rabbit.
1 cup of plain flour.
Bunch of fresh herbs (parsley, thyme, rosemary).
Salt.

Black pepper.
1ltr bottle of vegetable oil.
2 eggs.
A good seeded or rustic wholemeal loaf of bread.
4 cloves of garlic.
Half a small chilli.

Prep

Tear off about 4 to 6 chunks of bread and place in a blender. Blitz roughly to allow more space. Add you fresh herbs, garlic cloves, chilli and a good grind of salt and pepper. Blitz until you have a fine to medium sized breadcrumb. Spread the breadcrumbs out on a plate or tray and leave to one side. Beat your eggs into a bowl. Slice your game into small/medium sized strips trying to keep them all a similar size. Pour the oil into a pan. Tip the flour onto a plate or tray.

Method

Turn on the heat and begin to heat up your oil, do not leave it unattended. While the oil is heating, cover the game in the flour. Then, cover thoroughly in the egg wash. Then do the same with the breadcrumbs, making sure you get as much on as possible. Once your oil is hot enough, you can test by putting a single goujon in, and if it starts to sizzle, then you're good to go. Start very carefully using a small ladle and put in your goujons. Using the metal ladle gently turn the goujons in the oil to ensure even cooking. Once the breadcrumbs have turned a lovely deep golden-brown take one out and cut it in half to ensure its cooked in the centre. Once cooked remove from the oil onto some kitchen roll to drain any excess oil.

"These are a fantastic side or snack, perfect for using up any left-over game and a perfect substitute for those famous processed bite sized chicken pieces. My family absolutely love them served with some classic tomato sauce or some curried mayonnaise"

Chargrilled veg

Ingredients

1 to 2 large handfuls of mixed raw veg (broccoli, cauliflower, peppers, courgettes etc).

1 teaspoon of paprika powder.

1 teaspoon of cumin powder.

Black pepper.

Sesame oil.

Prep

Take your selection of veg and cut into slices roughly half a centimetre thick. Put all the sliced veg into a mixing bowl, drizzle with sesame oil and season with black pepper, paprika and cumin. Gently mix ensuring all the veg is covered with the seasoning and oil.

Method

Using a griddle pan on a medium heat or a grid over an open fire, simply place your veg spread out on the grid (no extra oil or butter needed) and cook gently. Keep an eye on it so not to burn it, but try to only turn the veg once or twice so reduce the chances of breaking the veg. Create some lovely, charred lines on each side. The veg is ready whenever you decide but its best served al dente with a nice crunch to it.

Sweet potato wedges

Ingredients

1 large, sweet potato (per serving).
Flaked sea salt.
Black pepper.
1 Teaspoon of paprika.
Garlic infused olive oil.

Sprig of fresh rosemary.

Prep

Do not peel but rinse your sweet potato using cold water and your hands. On a chopping board, cut your potato into full length wedges, you should get 6 – 8 wedges per potato. Put your wedges into a mixing bowl and add a good drizzle of the garlic oil some salt and peeper and the paprika. Mix together, ensuring an even covering. Chop your rosemary and leave to one side.

Method

Add another small drizzle of the oil to a non-stick pan on a medium to high heat and add your wedges. Toss the pan, ensuring the wedges are moved around until they have some colour on each side and start to soften. Turn the heat down and cook for a further 5 minutes. Now add your chopped rosemary to the wedges and toss a couple more times, before placing the oven safe pan into a Preheated oven for about 15 – 20 minutes until you have a soft potato with a slight crispy and full of flavour skin. Once out the oven, sprinkle with a little more flaked salt ready to serve.

" These sweet potato wedges are a great accompaniment with so many dishes and a perfect alternative to using normal potatoes. "

Onion rings in beer batter

Ingredients

1ltr of vegetable oil.
150g of self-raising flour.
3 tbsp cornflour.
200ml (1/3pt) beer.

3 white onions.
Good pinch of flaked sea salt.

Prep

Slice and separate the onion into rings. Combine the flour and cornflour in a mixing bowl. Whisk in enough beer to make a smooth paste, then continue adding beer, gradually, until the batter is smooth and creamy, similar consistency to pancake batter.

Method

Heat the oil in a large pan over a medium-high heat until it reaches 180°C on a cooking thermometer (alternatively test the temperature by dropping a cube of bread into the oil – it should turn golden in 30 seconds).

Dip the onion rings, one at a time, in the batter. Shake off the excess, and then carefully fry for 4-5 minutes, turning occasionally until crisp and golden. Do this in small batches to avoid crowding the pan, allowing the oil to come back up to temperature between frying each batch. Drain on kitchen paper. Serve immediately adding a sprinkle of flaked sea salt on top.

Damper Bread on the campfire

Ingredients

1 cup of self-raising flour.
1 tsp of sugar.
1 tbsp of butter.
½ - 1 cup of water.
Pinch of salt.

2 green sticks or skewers.
Sweet addition of your choice, chocolate spread, honey, jam etc.

Prep

If using sticks, prep them by rinsing them in cold water and whittling a point at one end. Get the children to do this under supervision.

Method

Rub the butter through the flour using your fingers until it is all crumbly. Mix in the salt, sugar, and a bit of water until it forms a dough. Divide the dough into 2 pieces and roll into the shape of snakes. Take the snakes and wind round the sticks/skewers. Hold the skewers over the campfire to cook until golden brown. Once cooked, leave to one side to cool and then remove the stick/skewer and fill the hole with your choice of sweetie goodness!

" These are very popular in Scouting, as they are an easy task for kids to do themselves in larger groups, often then enjoyed sat round the fire with a cup of hot chocolate and singing campfire songs."

Bruschetta with mozzarella

Ingredients

100-125g mozzarella ball.
1 long rustic loaf/baguette.
Large handful of fresh basil.
Good glug of quality extra virgin olive oil.
Black pepper.

1 large garlic clove.
Splash of balsamic.
Fresh vine tomatoes, the amount needed will depend on the variety you use.

Prep

Using a sharp knife, dice the tomatoes and mozzarella into equal small bitesize cubes, being delicate with the tomatoes trying not to squash them, then place them in a bowl. Slice the basil into nice thin strips getting rid of any stalks and add to the bowl. Cut the baguette at an angle, aiming for a nice couple of inch thickness per slice. Peel your garlic clove and slice off one end so its flat.

Method

Using a dry griddle pan, start to toast your bread until it's slightly crispy, with scorch lines on each side. Once toasted, place on a chopping board and use the garlic clove to rub over each side of the toasted slices to add flavour. Lay all your slices out and give them a quick drizzle of the olive oil. Now, top your slices with the mixture of basil, tomatoes, and mozzarella. Finish of by adding a grind of black pepper and a quick drizzle of balsamic vinegar.

" This dish is all about the produce. Fresh, quality and in season will turn a good bruschetta into an amazing bruschetta."

Sweets

Smoors

By the campfire

Ingredients

Bag of medium sized marshmallows.
1 packet of chocolate digestive biscuits.

Prep

Build and light your campfire, ensuring you have cleared the area well of any extra combustible materials and you are in a safe area which won't cause any damage to wildlife habitats or the environment and adequate water is available to extinguish when needed. You will need a skewer, which you can get from the kitchen, but I think its much better and great for the kids to get involved in if you make your own by getting a thin green stick and use a knife to sharpen one end creating a natural skewer that you can burn afterwards.

Method

All you need to do is put your marshmallow on the end of your skewer and toast over the fire until you have your chosen level of toasted. I like to categorise these into barely warm, golden, slightly crispy, chard, and on fire! Once you have toasted it, take 2 biscuits and with the chocolate side facing each other use them to grab the marshmallow and pull off the skewer forming a gooey and sticky sandwich that will always leave you wanting some more, hence the word 's'mores'

"Another campfire favourite for children and adults to enjoy."

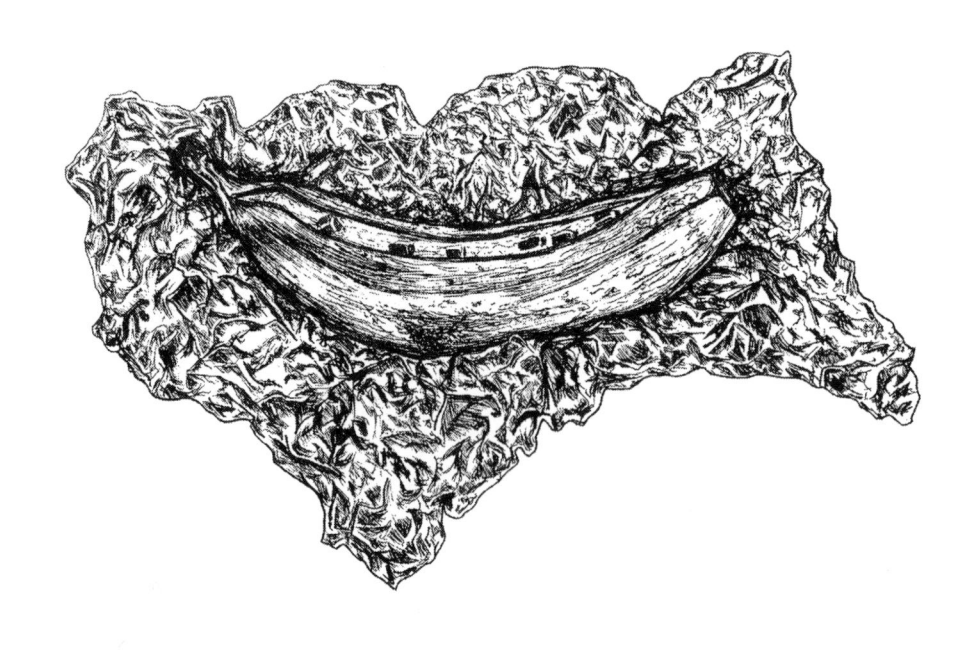

Fire-baked chocolate bananas

Ingredients

Two bananas.
1 bar of your favourite chocolate.
Splash of brandy or Cointreau.

1 scoop of vanilla ice cream.
Kitchen foil.

Prep

Preheat the oven or light your BBQ and let it die down. Keep the bananas in their skin and cut through one side of the skin and the banana, but not through the other skin. Roughly break up your chocolate bar or snap into cubes.

Method

This really is a very simple but tasty recipe that always goes down well with both children and adults. Where you have slit the banana on one side, stuff in your chocolate (you could add mini marshmallows as well). Place the bananas in some kitchen foil and lift the edges slightly. For the adults, splash over some brandy or Cointreau, or you can use orange juice or honey for if you need it alcohol free. Now bring up the foil side and scrunch together at the top forming a parcel. After about 10 minutes you can remove from the heat. Leave to cool for a min or two. You can put the foil parcels straight onto a plate and eat straight out of the banana skin, but not before adding a generous scoop of ice cream and grated chocolate.

" What a fantastic way to get one of your 5-a-day with the added extra of chocolate and ice cream, and better still, no washing up!"

Biscoff popcorn pudding jar

On a cliff edge

Ingredients

- 1 handful of popcorn kernels.
- Nub of butter.
- 4 Biscoff biscuits.
- 1 banana.
- 2 plain or chocolate sponge cupcakes.
- Jar of Biscoff or cookie spread.
- 1 tbl spoon of chopped almonds.
- 1 tbl spoon of chopped pistachios.
- 1 empty clean jar big enough to fit a dessert spoon in.

Prep

Roughly break-up your biscuits or smash with a rolling pin into a mixing bowl. Break your cupcakes into small bitesize pieces and add them to the bowl.

Method

Using a pan on a medium heat or two sieves clipped together over an open fire, add the nub of butter and your kernels and toast until they have all popped. You must constantly shake the pan/sieve to not burn the popcorn. Take off the heat and leave to one side. Gently toast your almonds and pistachios in a dry pan, then add to the popcorn to cool. Peel and slice your banana. Take your bowl of cakes and biscuits, add the nuts, banana, and most of the popcorn, and gently mix together so you don't mush the banana. Place the mixture into your jar, but don't compress it; it will need some gaps. Add 3 to 4 generous tablespoons of the spread in a saucepan and heat very gently until it has become a liquid. Pour most of the sauce gently over your mix, add some more popcorn, then drizzle with a little more sauce.

" You can eat this while it's still warm or leave to cool, either way, it's delicious! "

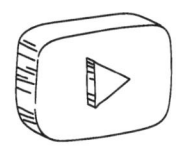

" Watch me cook this on YouTube "

Channel: Wildernessrobbo | **Play list:** Cooking in the wild
Video: Biscoff pudding jar

Mum's Flapjacks

Ingredients

8oz butter.
6oz Demerara sugar.
6oz syrup.
1lb oats.
Drop of vanilla essence.

Feel free to add into the oats a handful of mixed dried nuts, seeds or berries.

Prep

Grease a square or rectangular non-stick oven tray and its sides.

Method

In a pan heat the butter, sugar and syrup gently until melted. Take off the heat and stir in your oats (plus your extra nuts/seed/berries) ensuring they are all fully coated. If they are not fully covered, you can always add some more syrup and butter. Pour the mixture into your tray and spread out evenly. Place in the middle of the oven and cook on a medium heat for around 20 to 25 minutes, or until golden brown. Remove from the oven and allow to cool before cutting into portions.

" My mum's flapjacks have been fuelling my outdoor adventures for years and are high in energy. Whenever I'm away with a group, I'm often asked if I'm bringing any of my mum's flapjacks for the adventure, although the truth is they've usually all been eaten on the car journey! "

Drinks

Utepils
(pronounced ooh-ta-pilz)

A Norwegian word meaning
"to enjoy a beer outside on a sunny day."

Pine Needle Tea

Ingredients

1 pint of water
Sprig of fresh pine

Note

Forage a fresh sprig of pine from as high up the tree as you can reach to avoid contamination from passing wildlife and dogs. Always ensure you are totally confident in your identification as some other tree species that may look similar like Yew, which are poisonous to consume.

Method

Rinse the pine sprig and place in your pan of water. Bring to boil slowly and simmer for a few mins to strengthen the taste.

" Pour into your mug and enjoy not only a hot drink but one that is full of natural antioxidants and high in vitamins A and C."

Ginger and Spiced Apple Tea

Ingredients

1 eating apple.
Fresh ginger.
1 pint of water.

Cinnamon stick.
4 cloves.
Tablespoon of honey.

Method

Slice off two thin pieces of apple and roughly quarter up the rest of it. Slice 3 to 4 bits of fresh ginger, leaving the skin on. Place all the apple and the slices of ginger into a pan. Add the pint of water, cinnamon stick and cloves and bring to boil. Turn down the heat, add your honey and simmer slowly for 4-6 minutes to infuse all the flavours together. Remove the two apple slices and place them into your mug when ready. Then, using a small sieve, strain the remaining liquid into your mug, catching the other ingredients. I recommend serving with a slice of good-quality carrot cake.

" Apple and ginger tea has many health benefits including improved digestion, boosting immunity, ease inflammation, regulates blood sugar and is an excellent antioxidant "

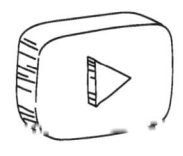

" Watch me cook this on YouTube "

Channel: Wildernessrobbo | **Play list:** Cooking in the wild
Video: Natural Remedy Spiced Apple and Ginger Tea

Mountaineers Hot Chocolate

Ingredients

1 shot of a good quality Scottish whisky (can make it a double shot if you wish).

1 mug of milk.

2 tablespoons chocolate powder.

1 teaspoon toasted marshmallow syrup.

1 medium to large marshmallow.

1 segment or mini snack-size Toblerone.

Squirty cream.

Method

In a small pan bring the milk to boil slowly and simmer on a low heat (too high a heat or fast boil can burn the milk and ruin it). Put 2 teaspoons of chocolate powder into your chosen mug and pour the hot milk over it, making sure to mix well with a teaspoon or mini whisk. Add the syrup, followed by the whisky. Drop in your segment of Toblerone to add an extra kick of mountain chocolatey goodness. Now toast your marshmallow until crispy and float on top, then to finish off, add your own 'snowy peak' of squirty cream.

" Whether you choose to do this at the top of a mountain sheltered in a snow hole, or safely back at base camp, I can guarantee this will fill you with a sense of euphoria as though your being hugged by a chocolate Santa Claus and kissed by a whisky flavoured fairy."

" Watch me cook this on YouTube "

Channel: Wildernessrobbo | **Play list:** Cooking in the wild
Video: The best hot chocolate ever

Summer Fruits mocktail

Ingredients

2 litres of lemonade.
1 bunch of fresh mint.
Tray of ice cubes.
6 - 8 slices of Cucumber.

Your choice of seasonal summer fruit (oranges, lemons, cherries, apples, limes, strawberries, pineapple, kiwi) etc.

Prep

Rinse all fruit, cucumber and mint with cold water.

Method

This one really is up to you, however I like to get a big glass jug and place in the fresh mint and cucumber. In no particular order, take my selection of fruit and put in a combination of pieces, zest/peel and freshly-squeezed juice from the fruit. Once you have added all the fruit you want. Pour in your lemonade. Finish with plenty of ice and leave for all the flavours to infuse before serving.

" This is a great one for the kids to do all by themselves, with supervision in using a knife, obviously. They can have a great time making this and feel grown up drinking cocktails with the adults. "

Sloe Gin

Ingredients

Roughly 500g sloe berries.
Roughly 250g caster sugar.
1 70cl bottle of gin.

If you wanted to experiment with your flavoured gin, you can try adding some other fruits, herbs or spices to your infusion. Damsons, almonds and cinnamon all work well with sloe berries for a twist on the usual flavour!

Prep

Sloe berries are the fruit of the blackthorn, so watch out for thorns when picking! Usually, sloes will start to be ripe enough to pick in early autumn; those that have ripened in the sunshine will be ready first and will also likely be sweeter than those that have grown in the shade. Be aware - as tempting as they look, sloes do NOT taste good raw and too many eaten raw can make you ill. You can freeze your berries until you're ready to make your sloe gin - in fact, freezing sloes makes their skins burst, which can help speed up the maceration process when you do start to make your liquid. It will take all of two minutes to prepare your homemade sloe gin; then all you need to do is wait! It will take at least four weeks for your gin to take on a really rich flavour and colour, and you can leave it for much longer if you wish – I would recommend up to three months, but many people leave their sloe gin for years!

Method

Pour all three ingredients in a sterilised glass jar, close and shake well.

Start with just enough sugar to cover the sloes. You can always taste the gin and add more sugar at a later date, if you prefer it a little sweeter.

Store the gin in a cool, dark place and make sure the lid is on tightly. Give the jar a good shake about twice a week to help the flavours infuse.

After four weeks, taste your gin and add more sugar if you like. If you want a gin with more depth of flavour, leave the sloes to steep for a few more weeks (or months - there are no strict rules). Once the gin is to your liking, strain the liquid through a muslin cloth and pour into a clean bottle.

Keep your sloe gin tightly-sealed in a cool, dark place and it will last for at least a month. Many people leave their sloe gin to mature for years before opening!

" Wherever you choose to drink your tipple, make sure you enjoy the fruits of your labour and patience it took to make. My personal favourite places are when working the dogs on a cold and frosty shoot day, or after a day on the winter mountains coming home to a roaring log fire, maybe a few roasted chestnuts and my favourite glass, filled with sloe gin. "

Rum and Pineapple Cocktail

Ingredients

Per cocktail,

1 slice of fresh pineapple, roughly 1inch thick.

1 cinnamon stick (optional).

Pineapple leaf.

1 tsp of brown sugar.

Couple of pinches of cinnamon powder.

1 handful of crushed ice.

1 shot of authentic Jamaican rum.

1 shot of pineapple rum.

Half a glass of fresh pineapple juice.

Prep

Cut your pineapple slice into 4 triangles (pie-shaped).

Using 3 of the pineapple slices, dice into small cubes, roughly 1cm squares. Place in a jug with a small pinch of cinnamon powder, a pinch of brown sugar and mix together.

Method

Using a griddle pan on a medium heat place the 4th slice of pineapple onto it along with the cinnamon stick. Sprinkle both sides with a pinch of brown sugar and cinnamon powder, leave on the heat until both sides of the pineapple have some nice scorch lines in and the sugar has caramelised and then remove from the pan and place to one side.

Pour the pineapple juice into the jug along with the two shots of rum. Using a tall glass half full with crushed ice, pour in your mixture from the jug. Garnish the glass by putting one slice in the middle of the pineapple triangle to slide onto the glass, then place the pineapple leaf as well as the cinnamon stick into the cocktail and use as a stirrer.

Extra Bits

Extra Bits

Game

Game is an animal not normally domesticated that is hunted for food. Ground game such as rabbits and squirrels, small birds, such as pheasant and partridge, and larger game such as deer are all hunted for food. Some game like grouse and the other small birds are often bred for sport hunting and has been long part of a very old tradition, although this has come under scrutiny over the more recent years. The majority of game can only be shot at certain times of the year, and you must have permission to shoot the game by the landowner. Depending on the type of game it's usually hung in a cold dark place for the required time and taste. Pigeons are often shot on a large-scale by farmers, or by people farmers have asked to come and shoot them to protect their fields of crop, which the pigeons come to in the hundreds to feed. Although pigeons don't have a lot of meat on them, their breast meat is fantastic shallow fried in a little butter, a dash of olive oil, a teaspoon of wholegrain mustard, a quick grind of pepper, then serve pink and garnish with a small handful of watercress.

Seasons

To get the best out of our ingredients its so important we take the season into consideration. For example, using seasonal winter veg like turnips and parsnips in a winter soup is important. Trying to source that veg during early summer will not only be very difficult to find, but its taste will also be poor and lacking in natural goodness. The taste of freshly shot partridge once the season is underway compared to a frozen one in the summer shot 4 months ago will be totally different. Picking your own seasonal fruit and veg has no comparison to packaged or frozen ones that have been packaged and preserved. As well as the superior taste of eating seasonal ingredients it also helps all our local farmers, small holders and local produces by buying local in-season ingredients.

Drinks

Never underestimate the importance of your choice of drink to accompany your meal. I personally feel people only ever talk about choosing the write drink when it involves wine, however I think it should go further and involve every possible drink option even including the much underrated still, cold tap water. The choice is always going to be personal to you and how you are feeling at the time but just don't let societies choice of white wine has to accompany fish and red wine should always be served with beef dictate your choice. I can't drink any larger when I eat as I find it too gassy, but I love a real ale with steak and chips in a beer garden or a large glass of freezing cold tap water if sitting down for a big Sunday roast at home. The choice is yours!

Animal Welfare

As I said at the start of this book, I am a very strong believer in understanding where meat and animal produce comes from and feel even stronger about passing that onto my children. We cannot change the world and how it produces food all on our own, however if you as an individual or household do your absolute best wherever possible to source responsibly, then combined that will go along way. We don't all have the room for large veg plots, fruit trees and chickens in the garden however we all have space for a plant pot of strawberries, or a bucket of potatoes and we can certainly do our own research on where to locally buy the most free-range chicken and eggs or line caught salmon and hand dived scallops. Visiting local farms and understanding a typical day will surprise most people but it's a great way to also learn about local produce. Whenever possible support your local farm shop and greengrocer and avoid the big supermarkets that fill their shelves with produce from all over the world often overlooking the damage that has not only on the environmental effects of transportation but different animal welfare laws in other countries.

BBQ

I absolutely love to BBQ my food, its where my love for cooking outside originally came from. There are now many different types of BBQs from high tech all singing all dancing gas BBQs, self-contained portable BBQs, to smokers, to traditional charcoal BBQs with lids. Here are a few of my personal tips to cooking on a traditional BBQ without a lid.

- Use a good quality charcoal.
- Line your tray with kitchen foil, it not only reflects the heat but helps when cleaning.
- Load the charcoal so there is a cooler area for when the food is almost done.
- Do not start adding your food until all the initial flames are out.
- Ensure your cooking grid isn't too wide. That sneaky sausage that falls through the gap is always a depressing site!
- Invest in a meat probe to check the internal temperature of the meat. They don't cost allot of money and really do ensure there is no accidental raw servings.
- If using burger buns, I think the better the bun the better the overall taste, so I like to buy a brioche bun and slightly toast it each side on the BBQ before serving the burger.
- Remember that just because it may look cooked on the outside doesn't mean its cooked in the middle.
- Stagger your cooking, different food takes different times, and it also helps by not overloading the grid.
- Don't rush! BBQs are a social event, and the food should be cooked the same way.

"If Barbecue did not exist, It would be necessary to invent it."

- Unknown genius.

Basic Bushcraft Fire skills for Cooking Outdoors

One of the most enjoyable parts of cooking wild for me is when I go back to basics and cook on an open flame from a campfire that I've built and started myself. The satisfaction of igniting that first flame from natural resources is amazing and I recommend everyone to experience it. Making a campfire with your children is always a great thing to do and another highlight of the year for me and the boys. I try to get them as involved as possible and at the same time they are learning life skills and respect for the fire and the possible dangers around it. There are many excellent books out there that focus purely on bushcraft and survival but as this book is all about "cooking wild" and cooking on naked flames I thought id share with you a few hints and tips to get you started.

- **Be safe!**

Whenever deciding to make a campfire ensure you are doing so in an area that does not cause damage to wildlife, woodland, moorland, private property. Make sure the fire can't spread out of control by making a safe barrier or boundary. Make sure you have plenty of water to extinguish the fire properly when done and never leave a fire unattended unless completely out.

- **Prepare!**

Before you get the fire lit, make sure you have enough fuel/wood to feed the fire. The last thing you want is to work hard getting the fire lit and then suddenly not have enough fuel to keep it going! When collecting your fuel only pick dead wood, preferably off the ground where is dryer. Arrange your wood in size order starting smallest/thinnest to biggest/thickest so it's easy to use.

- **Fire Lighters!**

Obviously, you can buy traditional fire lighters or the more natural compressed shavings, however there are many ways to start a fire using what nature provides. Fire by friction (the most common way): It requires you to rub wood together using a bow, or a hand drill.

Sparks: Using materials like rocks, flint, and a battery with wool is a standard way to create sparks that will start a fire.

Sun: Concentrating the sunlight to generate enough heat to make a fire is a less conventional method, but it can work if you have the right materials and weather conditions.

Chemicals: You can carry select chemicals that will combust when they are mixed. This is the least common method because of the hazards of having to take potentially combustible materials on the trail.

- **Fuel!** The best wood to burn on campfires and to cook over are clean burning and slow burning hardwoods such as Oak, Ash, Birch and most fruit trees. When choosing a coal to cook over, do your research. Some types of coals burn hotter and faster, some burn slower and produce less heat, some are totally organic and some you can use several times. All I would recommend is don't just choose the cheapest as there is usually a reason for it and secondly, I personally would completely ban buying the disposable BBQ's. They are the cause of so many wildfires, scorch marks and litter across the countryside and they are also pathetic in terms of quality.

> "fire-wood makes you warm three times; first collecting it, secondly shifting it and third when you burn it."
> – Ray Mears.

Kit List

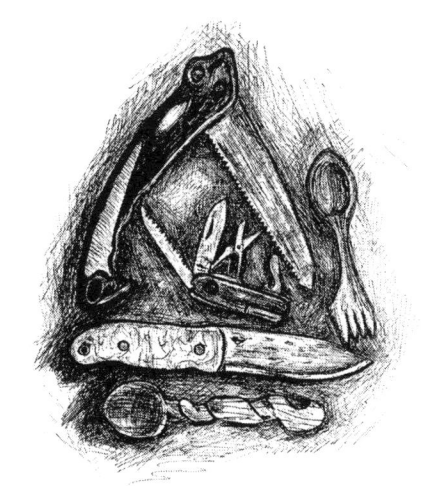

Tools & Utencils

Fire Starting Kit

Pans & Skillets

Stove & Kettles

Outdoors vs Epilepsy

Part of my love for the outdoors and the adventures I have in it, like cooking, is down to being diagnosed with epilepsy when I was 16.

I had my first seizure totally out of the blue as I was getting ready early one morning to go abroad with some friends to celebrate finishing school. That resulted in me missing the holiday and was the start of a very tough couple of years full of hospital appointments, GP appointments, nurse appointments, neurologist appointments, all different types of scans and tests, various medications, as well as a couple more seizures. I was told by one neurologist that I'd never be able to drink alcohol, go to nightclubs, join the military or other uniformed services, probably would never drive, avoid flashing lights, be on medication for the rest of my life and generally painted an awful future for me. Bearing in mind, I was a 16-year-old lad who'd just finished school with a place at college, and let's be honest, all I thought about was having a good time with my mates, trying to get into town for nights out and meeting girls. Now I felt it was all over. I felt I was some 'weirdo' that no girl would want to be with, and I had no future!

Luckily, and some might say remarkably coincidentally, my mum had recently become an epilepsy nurse specialist and, along with my dad, not only played a massive part in helping me through the diagnosis but also was influential in getting a second opinion from other neurologists, who in time painted a much more acceptable and promising future. The outcome was the same; I was epileptic. However, they took away all the doom and gloom and old-fashioned approach of the first neurologist and gave me some hope of positive outcomes and possibilities.

"Walking is a man's best medicine".
Hippocrates.

During the first couple of years, I really struggled mentally to deal with my diagnosis, and as I was now slightly more restricted to where I could go, I found myself spending most of my spare time walking my dog, a Border

Collie called Dan. It started by just walking up to a local field and then further to woodlands and nature reserves. Then I would get a lift up to our local moorlands, where I would be dropped off with Dan for a long walk and picked up when done. These walks and adventures in the wilderness soon became my medicine and no matter how I felt when I left the house at the start of the walk, I knew that during it and after, for a period of time I would be happy, my mind and thoughts would be free of stress and worries and filled with positivity and appreciation for what was around me. I often just found a place to sit down, breathing in the fresh, clean air with Dan at my side and listen to the ground birds chirping, the red kites calling each other, the sheep and cows doing their thing and watching as wildlife went about its business. No medication I'd been prescribed made me feel good, but this did. This made me feel well, this made me feel positive, this made me feel healthy, this was the wilderness, this was the great outdoors, this was the best medicine ever, and this was what I needed to motivate me to turn my life around and not let epilepsy win!

"Don't let anyone define you. You define yourself".
Billie Jean King.

Since then, I've made it my mission to inspire others who have been diagnosed with epilepsy by trying to achieve as many of the things I was told I couldn't/shouldn't do by that first neurologist. After finding the right medication for me and being seizure-free for one year, I did an intensive driving course and passed the first time. I went on to set up and run my own successful landscaping and grounds maintenance company, which I did for roughly 20 years. I do not have photosensitive epilepsy, so I had many Friday or Saturday nights in the pubs and clubs. I do drink, but sensibly and in moderation. I met my wife Becky and we have a fantastic, loving family together. In 2020, I applied to be an on-call firefighter for my local town. I went through all the tests, exams and training and passed the course. After nearly three years of being on-call, I also decided to apply to be a full-time firefighter for Derbyshire Fire and Rescue, which was an extremely hard process to even get an interview. However, I did get offered the role subject to passing the training course. The training was 16 weeks of relentless hard work, both physically and mentally, but I passed the course along with my other new recruits and was also awarded the teamwork award, which I'm very proud of. At the time of writing this, I believe I am the first and only operational serving firefighter in the UK to have epilepsy, which hopefully inspires others. Whilst in the service, I've competed in the national three peaks in full fire 'kit', raising money for charities and continued to have many adventures in the woods, moorlands and mountains, climbing, walking, mountain biking, wild camping, wild swimming and of course cooking in the wild.

I don't list these achievements to brag and boast, I list them to show others that it's possible to break down barriers, make your own future, to never give up, to prove that hard work and determination pays off, never take no for an answer and don't always accept what card life has dealt you!

As an ambassador for Epilepsy Research UK, I hope I can help people struggling with this condition by hearing my story and finding their own motivation, as I did in the great outdoors.

RESULT

OUTDOORS 1 vs EPILEPSY 0

My favourite Peak District walk

Spending nearly all my life in Chesterfield, Derbyshire, having the Peak District on my doorstep, I have spent many Sundays out on walks enjoying what the countryside has to offer yet out of all the beautiful walks and landmarks in the Peak District I have one route that is by far my favourite and the one I have walked more than any other.

I want to share this route with you, not because it's a secret, far from it but I want to share its true beauty, my personal memories and the things that walking there for over 30 years has enabled me to discover.

Curbar Gap

Curbar Edge is a surprisingly stunning spot just a stone's throw from Sheffield and a great spot for a family walk. The Curbar edge walk starts at Curbar Gap. Walk along the top of Curbar edge enjoying views over the Derwent valley and moorlands.

Curbar Edge + Froggatt Edge Walk

Walk Start: Curbar Gap Car Park

Walk End: Curbar Gap Car Park

Walk Distance: 8 miles

Hiking Time: 3.5-4 hours

Total Ascent: 263 m

Ordnance Survey Map: OL24 White Peaks – Peak District

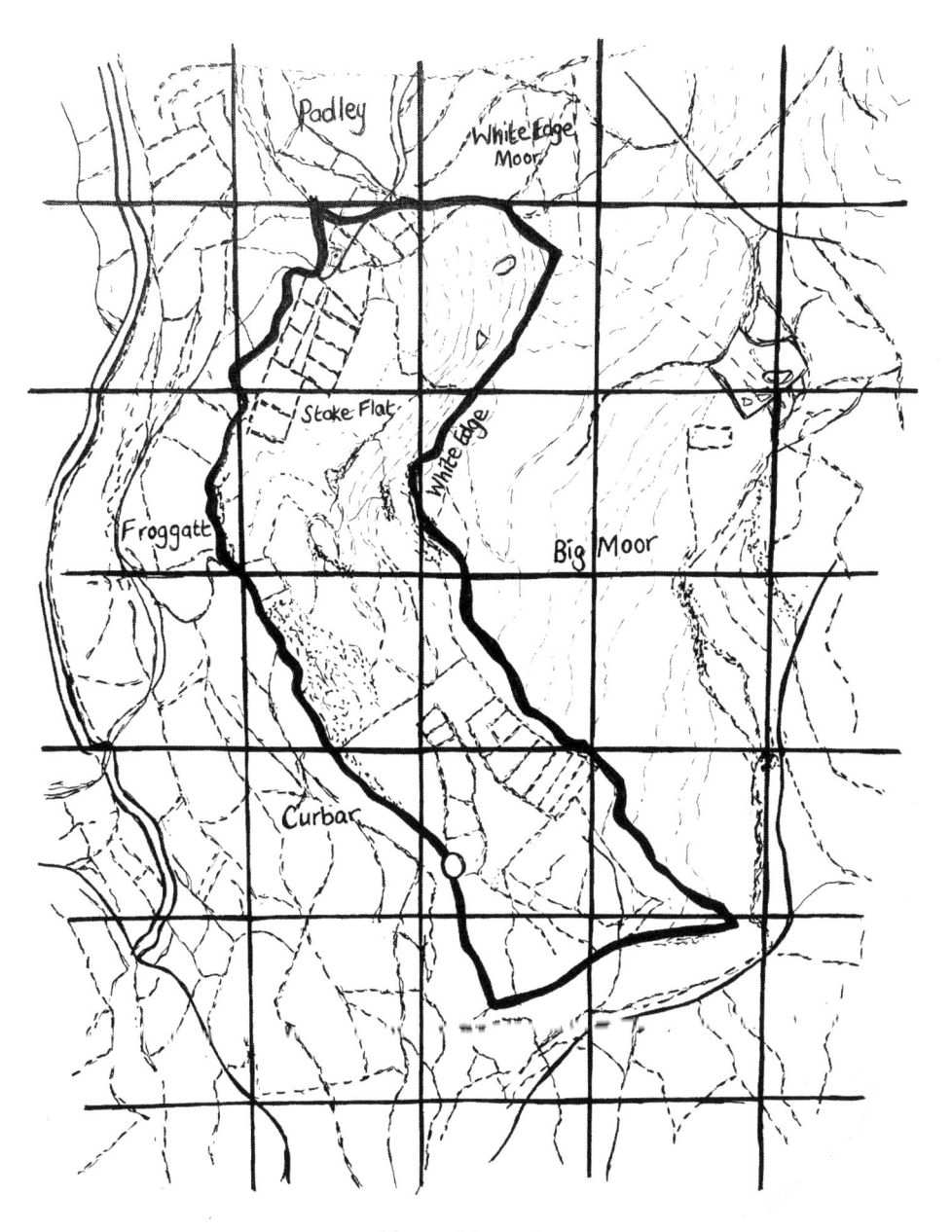

Map not to scale.

Curbar Edge to Froggatt Edge

Walk Stage 1

Highlights:
The amazing views from the Edge, Red deer and the Stone Circle
Start by walking out the far end of the car park, where you'll see a sign for Curbar Edge.

This takes you straight up to the Edge literally straight away. That's the beauty of the walk, within a few minutes you already have beautiful views. There's a footpath but if you prefer you can walk closer to the rocky edge for some even more epic views!

From Curbar Edge, you descend a rocky path which then continues onto Froggatt Edge.

In autumn, the colours look stunning, reds and oranges blended in with the rocks. Look out for movement amongst the trees as you might see deer camouflaged amongst the trees and bushes.

The area is popular with rock climbing so you might see people climbing down the sheer rocks along the route.

This walk includes a section of path that runs alongside open moorland and a section of woodland trail. The flora and fauna varies throughout the year. Visit in August for purple heather. June/July are good seasons to see the ferns growing thickly in the area.

On this walk you may be able to see purple heather, fox gloves, European ferns, wool grass, bilberry plants, hares, pheasants and grey squirrels.

About 2 km into the walk, on the right-hand side you'll see a Stone Circle, it's still intact with the stones clearly standing in an opening surrounded by trees. A short distance after this there's a small stream that runs downhill.

You can explore further down here if you want and after heavy rain, you might be lucky enough to see a little waterfall.

Froggatt Edge to White Edge

Walk Stage 2

Highlights:
More gorgeous views from the edge, deer rutting in October
The path winds downwards until you reach a road, from here you hike past the Grouse in and up.

Finally, reaching the path which takes you along White Edge, which runs parallel to Froggatt and Curbar Edge. In October, listen out for the sounds of the deer rutting, they are unbelievably loud, and you can hear them along the entire edge. Look out for them amongst the trees although they are hard to spot unless they are moving. I have wild camped along White Edge many times specifically in the rutting season, observing and listening to the deer from a relatively close but safe distance.

Top tip
Take some binoculars and maybe a brown or camo coat, for a better chance of spotting the deer in the trees.

Walking along White Edge you can enjoy beautiful views of the Big Moor to your left (I sometimes take a detour to the small body of water on Big Moor for some wild swimming) and to your right there is the footpath and views from the start of your walk. There are a few great spots to stop for lunch along this section, large rocks that make great seats!

White Edge to Curbar Edge

Walk Stage 3

Highlights:
Views of the first section of the walk, Red Deer and trig point bagging
After about 2 km you can detour slightly to reach the trig point, at 365 m, if you like trig point bagging, or just continue along the path. The views are better if you keep to the edge of the path.

Just under 1 km from the trig point, you'll reach a sign which points you Right to Curbar Edge or straight on to Birchen Edge. Then take the path for less than 1 km which will take you directly back to Curbar Gap Car Park.

If you would like to extend your Peak District walk, then continue your walk for an additional 2 miles then continue following the instructions below.

White Edge to Baslow Edge

Walk Stage 4

Highlights:
Highland Cattle and Wellington's Monument.
If you are happy to continue, then keep straight following the path. For some reason, on the OS maps the footpath doesn't show but if you're an experienced hiker you'll get to realise that not every path is on the map!

Follow the path for about 1 km where you reach the road. Cross the road and continue back onto the footpath through the gate (take note of the beware of the bull sign). If you're nervous of cows, like me, then you might be a little concerned. However, there is no need to be. In this field, there is usually a whole herd of beautiful Highland Cattle so please keep your dog on a lead.

The wonderful thing about these Highland Cattle is that they are so chilled out, sat relaxing, eating grass they look like they don't have a worry in the entire world! Once you've taken a few selfies and photos, it's time to continue walking up the path, with the woodlands on your left-hand side. There were lots of Highland Cattle hiding in the woods too so look out for them and their funny tree scratching habits! When you reach a large rock with a stone cross, you'll have reached Wellington's Monument.

Baslow Edge to Curbar Edge

Walk Stage 5

Highlights:
Eagle Stone, Baslow Edge and views of Curbar Edge
Take the footpath on your right, heading north back to your start point, about 50 metres ahead will be the iconic Eagle Stone. I admit I'm not 100% sure why it's called Eagle Stone, as, in my opinion, it looks nothing like an eagle.

I've been told that there's a rumour that many moons ago, men were challenged to climb to the top of the rock to be worthy of marrying the local maiden.

Again, similar to the path at the beginning of the walk along the Curbar Edge section, you can walk on the footpath or there's another path that follows Baslow Edge along a more rocky route. This has fantastic views initially over the grounds of Chatsworth and then into the valley. Its this specific spot that I scattered 'Dan' my faithful border collies ashes. We used to walk up here every week and was his favourite place to run and is another reason this walk is so special to me.

From here you simply follow the path down to the road, turn right and walk for a short section on the road back to the car park.

Watch me walk this on YouTube

Channel: Wildernessrobbo | **Play list:** wilderness adventures
Video: Curbar edge

Bonus Recipe
The Best Sandwich Ever!

Ingredients

Two large slices of good quality bread I use sour dough or Ciabatta.

Any left-over meat and veg from your Sunday or Christmas dinner.

Large nub of butter.

A good cup full of left-over gravy. You can always make fresh if you have non left.

Dash of good olive oil.

Prep

Cut all the vegetables so they are roughly the same size and slice the meat thinly and into bite size pieces.

Method

Using a large non-stick pan on a medium heat add a nub of butter, a small dash of olive oil and all your veg and trimmings. Stir fry for roughly 5 mins until piping hot. Now add your meat and mix with the veg for a couple of minutes. Add your gravy, stir well and simmer until the gravy has reduced right down before removing from the heat. Take your sliced bread and very lightly toast on a griddle or in the oven just to firm it up enough to hold the filling. Place your warm bread on a chopping board and load that bad boy up with all those great tasting left over meat and veg. Place the other slice of bread on top and with a good bread knife cut in half.

"Find somewhere to sit weather it be under a big comfy tree or your favourite armchair and grab a napkin because you're going to dribble this down your chin. Take that first bite and enjoy tasting every amazing ingredient in there. Once you've done you only have one thing left to do, fall into a deep sleep dreaming of what amazing meal you're going to cook next."

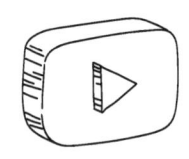

"Watch me cook this on YouTube"

Channel: Wildernessrobbo | **Play list:** Cooking in the wild
Video: The best sandwich Ever!

Bonus Recipe
Dutch Oven Cowboy Chilli

Ingredients

2 kg lean minced beef.
1 large white onion chopped.
2 cans of chopped tomatoes.
Half or a whole chorizo sausage.
1 bottle of dark beer.
2 good squeezes tomato puree.
1 can of mixed beans, drained. (Red kidney beans/pinto beans/cannellini beans/borlotti beans/haricot beans).
2 Jalapeno peppers.
2 green peppers.
3 to 4 level tsp of hot or mild chilli powder.
1 tsp cumin.
2 tsp oregano powder.
2 tsp paprika or smoked paprika.
Salt and pepper
4 cloves of garlic
2 spring onions.
Grated cheese.
Good dollop of sour cream.

Prep

Roughly chop the onion, chorizo and spring onion. Finely chop the green peppers, jalapenos and garlic.

Method

In a large pot or 12" Dutch oven brown the mince over a medium high heat. Season with salt and pepper or seasoning of your choice, to taste. As the meat begins to brown, stir in the onions and chorizo. Continue cooking until the meat has fully browned and onions are tender. If there is a lot of excess grease, drain. Stir in the chopped tomatoes, beer, tomato puree, beans and all peppers. Stir in the seasonings. Adjust taste, if needed.

Cover and cook over medium-high heat until it reaches a boil. Boil a couple minutes. Reduce heat and simmer for about 40-60 minutes, stirring occasionally ensuring it doesn't stick to the bottom and burn.

"I like to top with cheese, spring onions, sour cream and a roasted corn on the cob on the side, obviously sat by the campfire before falling asleep under your cowboy hat and the night stars."

A guide to seasonal fruit and veg

January

Apples, Pears

Beetroot, Brussels Sprouts, Cabbage, Carrots, Celeriac, Celery, Chicory, Jerusalem Artichokes, Kale, Leeks, Mushrooms, Onions, Parsnips, Spring Greens, Spring Onions, Squash, Swedes, Turnips

February

Apples, Pears

Beetroot, Brussels Sprouts, Cabbage, Carrots, Celeriac, Chicory, Jerusalem Artichokes, Kale, Leeks, Mushrooms, Onions, Parsnips, Purple Sprouting Broccoli, Spring Greens, Spring Onions, Squash, Swedes

March

Rhubarb

Artichoke, Beetroot, Cabbage, Carrots, Chicory, Cucumber, Leeks, Parsnip, Purple Sprouting Broccoli, Radishes, Sorrel, Spring Greens, Spring Onions, Watercress

April

Rhubarb

Artichoke, Beetroot, Cabbage, Carrots, Chicory, New Potatoes, Kale, Morel Mushrooms, Parsnips, Radishes, Rocket, Sorrel, Spinach, Spring Greens, Spring Onions, Watercress

May

Rhubarb, Strawberries

Artichoke, Asparagus, Aubergine, Beetroot, Chicory, Chillies, Elderflowers, Lettuce, Marrow, New Potatoes, Peas, Peppers, Radishes, Rocket, Samphire, Sorrel, Spinach, Spring Greens, Spring Onions, Watercress

June

Blackcurrants, Cherries, Gooseberries, Raspberries, Redcurrants, Rhubarb, Strawberries, Tayberries

Asparagus, Aubergine, Beetroot, Broad Beans, Broccoli, Cauliflower, Chicory, Chillies, Courgettes, Cucumber, Elderflowers, Lettuce, Marrow, New Potatoes, Peas, Peppers, Radishes, Rocket, Runner Beans, Samphire, Sorrel, Spring Greens, Spring Onions, Summer Squash, Swiss Chard, Turnips, Watercress

July

Blackberries, Blackcurrants, Blueberries, Cherries, Gooseberries, Greengages, Loganberries, Raspberries, Redcurrants, Rhubarb, Strawberries

Aubergine, Beetroot, Broad Beans, Broccoli, Carrots, Cauliflower, Chicory, Chillies, Courgettes, Cucumber, Fennel, French Beans, Garlic, Kohlrabi, New Potatoes, Onions, Peas, Potatoes, Radishes, Rocket, Runner Beans, Samphire, Sorrel, Spring Greens, Spring Onions, Summer Squash, Swish Chard, Tomatoes, Turnips, Watercress

August

Blackberries, Blackcurrants, Cherries, Damsons, Greengages, Loganberries, Plums, Raspberries, Redcurrants, Rhubarb, Strawberries

Aubergine, Beetroot, Broad Beans, Broccoli, Carrots, Cauliflower, Chicory, Chillies, Courgettes, Cucumber, Fennel, French Beans, Garlic, Kohlrabi, Leeks, Lettuce, Mangetout, Marrow, Mushrooms, Parsnips, Peas, Peppers, Potatoes, Pumpkin, Radishes, Rocket, Runner Beans, Samphire, Sloes, Sorrel, Spring Greens, Spring Onions, Summer Squash, Sweetcorn, Swiss Chard, Tomatoes, Watercress

September

Blackberries, Damsons, Pears, Plums, Raspberries, Rhubarb, Strawberries

Aubergine, Beetroot, Broccoli, Brussels Sprouts, Butternut Squash, Carrots, Cauliflower, Celery, Courgettes, Chicory, Chillies, Cucumber, Garlic, Kale, Kohlrabi, Leeks, Lettuce, Mangetout, Marrow, Onions, Parsnips, Peas, Peppers, Potatoes, Pumpkin, Radishes, Rocket, Runner Beans, Samphire, Sloes, Sorrel, Spinach, Spring Greens, Spring Onions, Summer Squash, Sweetcorn, Swiss Chard, Tomatoes, Turnips, Watercress, Wild Mushrooms

October

Apples, Blackberries, Elderberries, Pears

Aubergine, Beetroot, Broccoli, Brussels Sprouts, Butternut Squash, Carrots, Cauliflower, Celeriac, Celery, Chestnuts, Chicory, Chillies, Courgette, Cucumber, Kale, Leeks, Lettuce, Marrow, Onions, Parsnips, Peas, Potatoes, Pumpkin, Radishes, Rocket, Runner Beans, Spinach, Spring Greens, Spring Onions, Summer Squash, Swede, Sweetcorn, Swiss Chard, Tomatoes, Turnips, Watercress, Wild Mushrooms, Winter Squash

November

Apples, Cranberries, Elderberries, Pears

Beetroot, Brussels Sprouts, Butternut Squash, Cabbage, Carrots, Cauliflower, Celeriac, Celery, Chestnuts, Chicory, Jerusalem Artichokes, Kale, Leeks, Onions, Parsnips, Potatoes, Pumpkin, Swede, Swiss Chard, Turnips, Watercress, Wild Mushrooms, Winter Squash

December

Apples, Cranberries, Pears

Beetroot, Brussels Sprouts, Carrots, Celeriac, Celery, Chestnuts, Chicory, Jerusalem Artichokes, Kale, Leeks, Mushrooms, Onions, Parsnips, Potatoes, Pumpkin, Red Cabbage, Swede, Swiss Chard, Turnips, Watercress, Winter Squash

Acknowledgements

I have faced many obstacles, hurdles and knockbacks in my life and writing my first ever book was no different! In total its probably took me 3 years to write, due to having issues with filming some of videos to go alongside the recipes, finance problems and general day to day life challenges with my day job and of course my most important role of being a dad and husband.

This nicely leads me into my first thankyou, my beautiful wife Becky, mainly because she is my constant, she supports me in whatever project, hobby, challenge I decide to take on, even the slightly crazy ones. I know she is at my side or at the end of a phone supporting me whenever I need her. I am very aware I'm not an easy person to live with sometimes, especially with when it comes to me living with Epilepsy and my job as a firefighter which has me working away from home allot, but when it comes to putting up with me and my ways, Becky you are simply my rock, thankyou and I love you.

Family is extremely important to me.

Becky and I have a stepdaughter and two sons together, Sydney, Samuel and Samson. Sydney your academic and independent streek makes me proud and I hope you read this book knowing that your academic intelligence and independence through life has helped push and inspire me to achieve some of my goals.

Samuel and Samson you are simply my proudest achievement in life, your zest for life, infectious laughs, caring and loving natures can pick me up when I'm away in the wilderness or struggling with what life may have thrown at me that day, you are my world and I thankyou from the bottom of my heart for being in my life.

Thankyou to my dad, after all, this book is dedicated to him and I know I would not have found my love for cooking and experienced professional kitchens without you so thankyou for opening this world to me and broadening my pallet, however you know the saying, behind every great man is an even greater woman! Mum, thankyou for everything you do for me and my own little family but also thankyou for being Dad's rock as I know you have been since you first met, you have, and are huge role models in mine and Steve's lives and given us both a benchmark to aim for.

Also a thankyou to my big brother Steve who along with his daughter Amelia has always been there to offer encouragement and support.

Thankyou to @chefslocker for suppling me with a Konro grill, an absolute excellent little, portable Japanese BBQ ideal to keep things safe and contained and at the same time suitable for cooking some amazing food on.

Some of the best Chefs in the world in the top Michelin starred restaurants choose the traditional Yakitori Grill over any other cooking method. Also known as a Konro or "Hibachi" Grill in the US, these grills can reach incredibly hot temperatures and stay hotter for longer.

Made from Diatomite (the fossilised remains of plankton) and mined traditionally by hand in Suzu Japan, the blocks are skilfully joined together without the use of mortar, for a stronger, tighter, and more fire-resistant finish. The Konro is then baked at 1,000 degrees for six hours making them extremely durable.

Because Diatomite Grills have superior heat insulation properties, charcoal used in them starts easily and burns for longer. Its composition and structure deflects heat back into the coals creating even heat distribution and very efficient cooking.

Konro Grills (sometimes also known as a shichirin) were originally developed in around the 8th Century A.D. and their original purpose was to act as a small room heater. Now they can be seen on just about every street corner in Japan.

Nothing tastes quite like charcoal grilled Yakitori or Kushiyaki. When cooked over Binchotan Charcoal, temperatures can reach up to 750c, juices instantly evaporate into a smoky cloud infusing any ingredient with an even char.

Chefslocker introduced the traditional Konro to the UK back in 2016 direct from the mines where they are still produced today.

Check out the grills and other items on their website
www.chefslocker.co.uk

Thankyou to Becky Hague, who has illustrated the drawings in this book. I've not made things easy for her, mainly down to the fact this is the first time I've wrote a book and although I knew what I wanted her to draw in my head, I couldn't always explain it properly, however somehow, she has done an absolute amazing job and put exactly on paper what was in my head!

About the Illustrator

Becky Hague

"As an artist my work is often inspired by people and nature, so when asked to help with this project I was delighted to be able to incorporate my love for food too!

I'm proud to be part of a project aiming to inspire more people to spend time outside and encourage healthy lifestyle choices. Being out in nature is a necessity for me – its where I feel relaxed, at peace and can enjoy adventuring with my husband and children. Having the chance to feel free and childlike, building dens and climbing rocks will never bore me.

As with everything I ever do, I have drawn every image with love and care, using my favourite media pen and ink. I honestly don't think there is anything better than the simplicity and rawness this media offers which is why I use this in most of my work. I do sometimes dabble in other media's such as alcohol inks, various types of paints and photography so please feel free to get in touch if you feel I may be able to assist you in any upcoming projects you may have. becky.hague@outlook.com.

Sending lots of love to you all as well as a massive shout out to my forever loving and supportive family and friends".

Notes

Notes

Notes

Notes

Notes

Notes

Notes

Notes

Notes